Problems of Teacher Education

Problems of Teacher Education

T.K. Hemchand

CRESCENT
PUBLISHING CORPORATION

Problems of Teacher Education

Edition : 2024

ISBN 978-81-8342-140-9

Published by:

CRESCENT PUBLISHING CORPORATION
4806/24, Mathur Lane,
Ansari Road, Darya Ganj,
New Delhi - 110002
Ph.: 011-23244131
Mob.: 9711991838, 9999021668
e-mail : crescentbook@gmail.com
Website : www.crescentpublishingcorp.weebly.com

Printed at :

Balaji Digital
Delhi

Preface

Teachers form the fulcrum on which the lever of education is supported. Not only are they indispensable to the learning process of the students, the interaction, motivation and discipline that they incorporate sustains the goals and objectives of education. No wonder then, that the education administration and management of a society or a nation takes ample consideration of the rigmarole of teaching and teachers before undertaking a crucial step. As the aspirations and opportunities offered by education widen, an issue also presents itself which carries great import for the educational endeavour that of teacher education.

Teacher education, or the training of teachers to equip them with the tools and skills to become effective educators, is not a new phenomenon. Nor are; however, the problems that persist within the purview of this endeavour even as they widen constantly. This book in the series on education problems tackles the issue of teacher education problem. Using a pragmatic approach to the matter, the book effectively delineates what entails the problems in the education of teachers, taking into account such issues as current political, social and cultural contexts, infrastructure, administrative rules, number of teachers, etc. It explores the problems through numerous perspectives critiquing the current situation, presenting forth numerous alternatives, and analysing the implications of these matters. It also studies teacher education systems within numerous educational systems, fostering a deeper understanding of the issue and enabling a better thought and action process to the Indian context.

It is hoped that the erudition and insight of the book serve well for the readers.

Prof. T.K. Hemchand

Contents

1

Teacher Education in India

India's commitment to the spread of knowledge and freedom of thought among its citizens is reflected in its Constitution. The Directive Principle contained in Article 45 enjoins that "the State shall endeavour to provide within a period of ten years from the commencement of this Constitution, for-free and compulsory education for all children until they complete the age of fourteen years'. Article 29 (1) provides that any citizen having a distinct language, script or culture will have the right to conserve it. Moreover, special care of the economic and educational interests of the underprivileged sections, particularly, the Scheduled Castes and Scheduled Tribes is laid down as an obligation of the State under Article 46.

In fulfilling these objectives, the role of the teacher must naturally be seminal, Apart from funding and building institutional structures, the diversity and complexity of India requires teachers of special vision and sensitivity, if the goals enunciated in the Constitution, specially pertaining to the underprivileged and the minorities are to be fulfilled.

National Policy on Education

Educational policy and progress have been reviewed in the light of the goals of national development and priorities set from time to time. In its Resolution on the National Policy on Education in 1968, an emphasis on quality improvement and a planned, more equitable expansion of educational facilities and the need to focus on the education of girls was stressed. It was also stated that of all the factors which determine the quality of education and its contribution to national development, the teacher was undoubtedly the most important. It was on the qualities and character, educational qualifications and professional competence of the teacher that success of all educational endeavours must, ultimately, depend.

About a decade and a half later, the National Policy on Education was formulated which was further updated in 1992. The NPE-1986 provides for a comprehensive policy framework for the development of education upto the end of the century and a Plan of Action (POA) 1992, assigning specific responsibilities for organising, implementing and financing its proposals. Among the distinguishing features and recommendations of this policy are:

- — emphasis on pre-primary education,
- — formulation of strategies based on micro-planning at the grassroots level to en-sure children's retention in school,
- — recommendation to lay down Minimum Levels of Learning (MLLs) for each stage of education,
- — integration of adult literacy and Non Formal Education (NFE) programmes with vital national concerns such as the small family norm, health care, environment and nutrition,
- — provision of essential facilities in schools,
- — adoption of a child-centred, activity-based approach, and

— establishment of District Institutes of Education and Training (DIETs) for the pre-service and in-service education of teachers for elementary schools and for personnel working in non-formal and adult education programmes.

In the NPE 1986, improvement in the status and professional competence of teachers is envisaged as the cornerstone of educational reconstruction. It emphasises that teacher education is a continuous process which new programmes of teacher education must reflect.

To ensure greater participation in education by all sections of society and also to improve quality, decentralised management structures are being introduced in states. This is in pursuance of the 73rd and 74th Constitutional Amendments of 1992 regarding Panchayati Raj and Nagar Palika institutions.

Education for All: International Policy and Programme Initiatives

The World Conference on Education For All (EFA) held at Jomtien, Thailand in 1990 affirmed the will of participating nations including India to meet the basic learning needs of all children, youth and adults. To achieve this objective a two-pronged strategy was designed, i.e., Universalisation of Elementary Education (UEE) and universal adult literacy, which has since been the priority policy and action areas for the participating nine highly populated countries.

Three years later in December 1993, India's commitment to EFA (Education for All) was reaffirmed in its adoption of the Delhi Declaration and Framework of Action at the EFA Summit. The Declaration calls for ensuring a place for every child in a school or an appropriate education programme according to his or her capabilities, consolidating efforts towards basic education for children, youth and adults from public and private sources, improving and extending literacy and Adult Education (AE) programmes within the context of an integrated strategy of basic education for all people, eliminating disparities of access to basic education, improving the quality and relevance of basic education, and in all actions and according to the highest priority at national and other levels, ensuring that a growing share of national and community resources is dedicated to basic education, improving the management of existing resources for education, and collaborating with other nations in the development of distance education.

At a Special Conference convened in February, 1994 following the summit, the Chief Ministers of all the States and Union Territories (UTs) decided that coordinated and concerted action would be needed on the part of the local community, state governments and the central government in the mobilisation of resources for education so that there was a substantial increase in budget allocation and so as to accord higher priority to primary and AE.

The process of affirmation of the goals of EFA was reinforced at the Mid Decade Review of EFA which took place in Amman, Jordan in June 1996, at which various initiatives were discussed in a country-specific context to review achievements of EFA.

Elementary Education

Making education accessible

Ensuring accessibility of educational opportunities has been the principal policy plank of governmental strategy. While special efforts were aimed at educationally disadvantaged groups, particularly, Scheduled Castes (SCs) (comprising roughly 17 per cent of the population) and Scheduled Tribes (STs) (constituting about 8 per cent of the populations), various measures including monetary and other incentives, and recruitment of more teachers from disadvantaged communities, and flexible school timings provided the fillip to the expanding coverage of enrolment. As an incentive to enrolment, attendance and retention, besides improving the nutrition of children, a nationwide mid-day meal programme has been launched during 1995-96. More than 33.5 million children benefitted from the scheme. By 1997-98 all government run/aided schools in the country would be covered.

The Indian education system is also unique in that it seeks to give due recognition and importance to the social organisation, traditions, customs and value systems of the various communities-particularly SCs and STs. This is supported by the development of materials and curricula in tribal languages, residential schools for tribal children and the encouragement of the young, educated members of the community to participate in the educational process.

Various initiatives have been taken to reduce the academic burden on students while improving the quality of education. Not only is curriculum development being decentralist but an increasing involvement of teachers in the development of textbooks, child-centred and activity-based method of teaching in schools and examination strategies are being formulated to assess the ability to understand rather than the ability to memorise. The system of examination, too, is continuously under review through introduction of continuous and comprehensive evaluation.

The Government, in 1996, has renewed its commitment and resolve to UEE and to spend atleast 50 per cent of the allocation on education which is to grow to 6 per cent of Gross Domestic Product (GDP) by the turn of the century as against the current level of about

3.23 per cent of GDP. Opening of residential schools for the poor children in each district and Teacher Housing Scheme are the thrust areas of the new policy.

New initiative: District Primary Education Programme

The District Primary Education Programme (DPEP) is the major initiative undertaken to effect improvement in the quality and UEE. The programme is distinguished by its holistic approach and the principle of contextuality in planning. This, in effect, implies that education is planned and organised in the specific context of the area concerned a shift from macro to micro planning with the district as the unit of planning. The programme lays great emphasis on people's participation and management, has a marked gender focus and seeks to enhance school effectiveness by increasing infrastructural facilities, developing instructional materials and training of teachers.

Non Formal Education

The NPE 1986, while taking the enormous challenge of achieving UEE in its entirety, recognised the fact that schools would not reach all children, particularly, millions of girls and working children whose participation in the school system is thwarted by socio-economic conditions. The Policy, therefore, called for a large and systematic programme of NFE as an integral component to achieve UEE with enough flexibility for learners to learn at their own pace and at the same time having quality comparable with formal education.

Secondary Education

In keeping with the role of secondary education in preparing students for further academic or professional studies, the policy has been focussed on improvement of quality through specific inputs such as the schemes for improvement of Science Education, Environment Education, Population Education and Computer Literacy. Government run schools, Kendriya Vidyalayas (Central Schools) have added to promotion of national identity throughout the country. The Government has accelerated the process of creating infrastructure and teacher training facilities so that these chains of schools act as pace setters for other schools in the country. Residential co-educational secondary schools [Navodaya Vidyalayas] have been established in each district to nourish talent in the rural areas. These schools have a positive bias in favour of girls and currently, about 1,20,000 students are enrolled on the basis of merit, in these schools.

Open School

A major initiative to expand access of education was to promote distance education. To this end, the Open School system also provides alternative schooling to neo-literates who have acquired functional literacy and also to dropouts from the school and the NFE systems so that their schooling continues of their own pace and at a time convenient to them. The National Open School (NOS) and the State Open Schools provide alternative means to acquire secondary level education in a flexible manner.

Vocational Education

Vocational education is the policy framework that seeks to provide diversification of educational options, increase potential employability and reduce the mismatch between demand and supply of skilled manpower. At present, about 10 per cent students take up vocational courses in the last two years of the schooling phase. The endeavour is that 25 per cent students be diverted to the vocational stream the end of the present century. A Central Institute of Vocational Education (CIVE) under The National Council of Educational Research and Training (NCERT) has been set up to support courses and develop instructional material. The Institute has accomplished this in about 150 vocations. It is also proposed to set up State Institutes of Vocational Education and strengthen existing ones. Pre-vocational education is being introduced at the lower secondary stage (classes IX and X). The scheme aims at covering 1,000 schools during the Eighth Plan (1992-97).

Non-formal vocational education and training programmes are also being introduced through Non Governmental Organisations (NGOs), specially, in rural areas. These are intended for girls in the 14-18 age group and are designed to emphasise entrepreneurship and introduce new and emerging technologies to women.

Higher Education

Higher education policy in India has been characterised by upgradation strategies that provide for quality improvement, and consolidation of facilities for existing Universities and Colleges. The higher education sector, considered vital for the national economy, has witnessed a steady growth since Independence in 1947. The enrolment of students too shows an increased share of women and SCs and STs in all stages of higher education. The utilisation of distance education as a cost-effective and easily accessible medium for upgradation of education and skills, particularly in remote areas, forms part of the thrust area in the higher education policy

Technical Education

Technical education is one of the most significant component of the human resource development spectrum with great potential for adding value to products and services, for contributing to the national economy, and for improving the quality of life of the people. In recognition of the importance of this sector, the successive five year plans laid great emphasis on the development of technical education. Technical education includes courses in engineering, technology management, pharmacy, applied arts and crafts, etc. Policy guidelines in technical education have sought to streamline courses and syllabi in 'relation to the manpower needs of the country as well as changing technological scenario across the globe.

Initiatives in Technical Education

Policy initiatives to revamp the technical education system include promoting institution-industry interaction, providing continuing education to update the skill and knowledge of technical personnel working in the industry and service sectors, the transfer of technology to the rural sector and setting up Technology Development Missions to meet the emerging challenges in science and technology.

In order to update and upgrade technical education in the Indian Institutes of Technology (IITs), Regional Engineering Colleges (RECs) and other institutions/polytechnics, obsolete machinery and equipment is weeded out, modern machinery and new equipment relevant to curricular needs introduced and opportunities for hands-on experience for students created.

A new policy measure has also been initiated to mobilise funds, particularly, for higher and technical education from non-governmental sources. In tune with the economic liberalisation of the economy, institutions are being encouraged to generate resources, raise fees which often have not been revised in the last three or four decades and embark on judicious financial management with the overall objective of reducing government subsidies.

A National Technical Manpower Information System has been developed by the Government to monitor the absorption of trained engineering and technical manpower and thereby, create a data base in order to streamline and plan the development of technical education.

During the past few years, the number of institutions in the private sector has increased considerably. A number of industrial houses have also established technical and management institutions. The government, however, has taken suitable measures to regulate education in the private sector to check its commercialisation and maintain standards through setting up All India Council of Technical Education (AICTE).

Adult Education

AE, an essential component of EFA is seen as an imperative for the growth of the individual and the nation. The National Literacy Mission (NLM), set up in 1988 with the goal of helping 80 million persons achieve literacy by 1995, has adopted the Total Literacy Campaign (TLC) as the dominant strategy for achieving its literacy goals. This has resulted in a rich and varied experience that has become an international resource. The Mission has now been extended to cover 100 million non-literates by 1997, that is by the end of the 8th Plan period.

Value-based Education

The NPE 1986 recognises that importance should be given to value-based curriculum incorporating the notion of an equitable society, secularism, democracy, and a scientific temper. These are reflected in the core elements of the school curriculum and also include observance of the small family norm, protection of the environment and gender equality. Human rights have also been now included. Both at the national and state levels, textbooks have been reviewed to eliminate passages that were inimical to human rights or that distorted them. Steps have, simultaneously, been initiated to include alternative material which shows sensitivity to human rights issues. Universities are also in the process of introducing courses on human rights. The NCERT has published a Source Book on Human Rights as a guide for teachers.

MEANS OF INSTRUCTION, EQUIPMENT AND INFRASTRUCTURE

The availability of textbooks, instructional material and infrastructure affects the quality of learning that the school system delivers. In a country like India, this takes on many dimensions both quantitative and qualitative. A number of efforts are, therefore, underway to ensure that the basic necessities of education are fulfilled.

Textbooks

School textbooks

By and large, textbooks remain the principal instructional material in the classroom. Thus, they assume great importance, especially, in contexts where for most students they are often the only reading material available. Efforts have, therefore, been made to ensure widespread availability of this critical educational input. Given that the Indian educational system enrols more than 100 million students in primary schools alone, it is significant that virtually all primary students have textbooks, with most receiving them in a timely manner, and at fairly affordable prices (the average primary text books are selling for about Rs.8, or about US$0.25).

At the national level, development of school textbooks often takes place, with the NCERT developing prototypes that are usually adapted or even adopted by states. Textbook publishing, however, is almost entirely in the hands of state agencies. The private sector too participates in varying degrees.

In most states, it is the SCERT that is responsible for textbook development, with a Textbook Corporation or Textbook Bureau that actually publishes textbooks. Typically, states publish textbooks for all the subjects, in all the significant languages of the state, with some states publishing hundreds of titles including books in more than 10 languages. It is in the printing and distribution aspects that the private sector is more involved, as in the case of states such as Uttar Pradesh, Maharashtra and Tamil Nadu. Some states, such as Madhya Pradesh, have set up regional depots and maintain computerised inventory control to ensure efficient distribution of textbooks.

With the textbook development and publishing capabilities in place, attention is now being turned to improvement in the quality of text-books. The Yash Pal Committee set up by the Government of India in March, 1992 comprised of experts who held extensive consultations across the country. In its report "Learning without Burden", the Committee has recommended decreasing the cognitive load that textbooks and curricula carry. Extensive studies pertaining to the readability of Indian textbooks have been undertaken by national institutions such as the NCERT and the Central Institute of Indian Languages (CIIL) and their outcomes are being utilised towards improvement.

With the introduction of the MLLs, the focus has shifted from information-based textbooks to competency-based ones. A number of Indian states are in various stages of developing new MLL-oriented textbooks and are working towards books that are learner-friendly and promote child-centred, activity-based learning. One significant development is the introduction of trialling, whereby, experimental textbooks are field tested before being introduced on a large scale.

Material for Non-Formal Education

Considerable work has been done by the NCERT towards the development of self-learning materials for primary level NFE programme. The main focus of this effort has been to design a set of innovative materials to facilitate the NFE instructors in handling multiability groups in diverse teaching-learning situations. The material includes coloured charts, comic books and textual materials in book form, covering the course in an integrated manner. A large number of classroom practitioners, subject experts and teacher educators participated in the development of this material.

The NCERT has also facilitated the development of integrated teaching-learning material based on MLLs for NFE in several languages, learner-specific material for street and working children and local-specific supplementary materials for NFE programme.

In addition to the NCERT, a number of NGOs too have been developing and using materials for the NFE centres being run by them.

Textbooks for higher education

In contrast to the school situation, textbooks for higher education are produced almost entirely by the private sector. The universities or institutions concerned specify their curriculum and recommend desirable texts. Indian publishers often receive financial assistance from the National Book Trust (NBT) towards publication of university level textbooks, particularly, medical textbooks. However, a significant proportion of textbooks used in higher education are either imports or Indian reprints and/or editions of foreign texts.

Scheme of Educational Technology

Under the centrally sponsored scheme of Educational Technology, TV sets and Radio-cum-cassette players are made available to upper primary and primary schools. So far, 62,000 colour TV sets and 0.36 million cassette players have been made available to schools. CIET and SIETs prepare instructional materials.

Computer Literacy and Studies in Schools (CLASS)

With a view to introducing computer literacy, CLASS scheme was introduced in 1984-85 under which about 4,000 Senior Secondary Schools have been covered.

Other instructional materials

Library facilities and teaching-learning material

Libraries are available in only one-fourth primary schools as against 90 to more than 90 per cent in secondary and higher secondary schools. Many states that have basic education projects (e.g. Rajasthan, Uttar Pradesh, Andhra Pradesh, Assam) have developed and disseminated supplementary reading material in addition to launching projects to initiate classroom libraries.

Private Schools

Facilities in private schools are better and teachers have greater access to them than in government schools. Effective utilisation of teaching-learning resources, however, remains limited to a small number of schools,

Audio-visual Material

With distance education programmes being telecast for

both school and higher education, a considerable repertoire of software is now available. The Central Institute of Educational Technology, under the NCERT, which has bee catering to the software and training requirements of school education in general, has recently shifted its focus to supporting primary education. The Institute has also undertaken initiatives for teacher training using satellite-based instruction for teachers. At the state level, similar responsibility is borne by State Institutes of Education Technology (SIETs). Man states (for example Karnataka and Himachal Pradesh) have provided thousands of schools with radio-cum-cassette-players which are use for audio programmes. A large scale programme initiated by the Space Application Centre (SAC), Ahmedabad, has developed software and broadcasts television-based educational programmes. A number of high schools across the country have been provide with television sets.

Operation Blackboard

Launched in 1987-88, this scheme aims to bring all primary schools to a minimum standard of physical facilities by providing them with :

— at least two reasonably large all weather rooms along with separate toilet facilities for boys and girls;

— at least two teachers and as far as possible one of them, a woman; and

— essential teaching and learning material including blackboards, maps, charts, a small library, toys and games for work experience.

Central assistance has been fully provided to all the targetted primary schools and the coverage is now being extended to upper primary schools. Primary schools with enrolment of more than 100 students and two teachers are now being provided with a third teacher.

So for, 5,30,000 schools have been covered under this scheme. The number of teachers' posts sanctioned is 1,52,000 (of which 1,43,000 posts have been filled up), while the number of classrooms to be constructed was targetted at 2,63,000 (of which 1,72,000 have been constructed). The expenditure on this scheme was Rs. 15152.9 million from 1987 to March 1995 and was Rs.2682.6 million during 1995-96.

Recent studies of students' learning achievement at primary level in selected districts revealed that charts, maps and globes are available in the blocks covered by the Operation Blackboard Scheme. The use of teaching aids, though, was reported by one-third or less teachers.

Classrooms

Given the large numbers of enrolment, there is no doubt a tremendous pressure on facilities available in schools. A visual on infrastructural facilities given above, indicates the availability of building and other facilities in different levels of schools.

Status of the Teaching Staff

The role of the teacher has been well recognised in the traditional Indian thought through the centuries. The 'Guru' (teacher) was to be revered as an imparter of knowledge and a guide. In the present context, the role of the teacher remains as critical as ever.

The teacher plays a major role in implementing the policies and schemes formulated to achieve a breakthrough in the quantitative expansion and qualitative improvement of education. Reflecting the crucial role of teachers in national development, the NPE 1986 called for a substantial improvement in the conditions of work and quality of teacher education.

The important determinants of the status of teachers could be identified as follows:

— The academic and professional requirements for entry into the profession
— The financial and other economic benefit
— The freedom of teachers to take part in public affairs
— The professional responsibility assumed
— The degree of public recognition.

Growth of the Teaching Profession

The teaching profession has the largest number of members as compared to other professions in India. During 1994-95, about 4.3 million teachers were working in different levels of schools. Of these, 2.7 million [66 per cent] were engaged in primary and upper primary schools [grades I to VIII] of which 2,01 8,050 teachers were in government schools. Of the 1.5 million [34 per cent] in high/higher secondary schools [grades IX to XII] 609,121 were in government schools.

During the period 1990-95, the total strength of teachers at different levels of school education increased from 4.0 million to nearly 4.3 million, marking an increase of 6.5 per cent. If this trend continues, the number of teachers, particularly primary and upper primary teachers, will grow significantly over the next decade.

A sex-wise analysis of the teacher force indicates that there are 3 times more male teachers than female teachers at all levels of school education. Although the number of female teachers has increased, yet, their share in the total teaching force is very small, particularly, in rural, remote and educationally backward areas. The number of women teachers in schools increased from 1,141,015 in 1987-88 (29.4 per cent) to 1,343,667 in 1993-94 (32.08 per cent).

System of Teacher Education

The NPE 1986, called for an over-haul of the Teacher Education System in the country. It emphasised the need for continuing education for teachers to meet the thrust envisaged in the policy. A new Centrally Sponsored Scheme of Restructuring and Reorganisation of Teacher Education was launched in 1987-88 which primarily envisages establishment of DIETs to provide pre-service and in-service training to elementary school teachers and to AE and NFE personnel. In addition, upgradation of Secondary Teacher Education Institutions into Colleges of Teacher Education (CTEs), establishment of Institutes of Advanced Studies in Education (IASE), strengthening of SCERTs and University Departments of Education through the University Grants Commission are components of this restructuring which has the basic objective of providing training and resource support to elementary and secondary education at the grassroots level.

Progress on teacher Education Schemes
Progress (As on 31st March, 96)

Sl. No.	*Item*	*Target*	*Achievement*
1.	Programme for Mass Orientation of School Teachers (1986-90)	2.0 million teachers	1.76 million teachers
2.	Establishment of DIETs	425 by the end of VII plan	424
3.	Upgradation of Secondary Teacher Education Institute into CTEs/IASEs	135	107
4.	Strengthening of SCERTs	All SCERTs	8
5.	Special Orientation Programme of Primary Teachers during 1993-97	1.8 million teachers	0.3 million teachers

Central assistance is meant for the construction of buildings, procurement of books and equipments, additional expenditure on staff salaries and training programmes. In view of the high priority accorded to the achievement of the target of UEE, emphasis under the Teacher Education Scheme has so for been on setting up of DIETs. It was proposed to establish DIETs in 425 districts in the country (as per 1987-88 configuration when there were 451 districts in total) by the end of the VIII Five Year Plan. Against this target, 424 DIETs have been sanctioned as on 31st March, 96. Seventy three CTEs and 34 IASEs have also been sanctioned. Eighteen SCERTs have been assisted under strengthening of SCERT component of the scheme.

Financial outlays for teacher education

(Rs. in millions)

Year	*Item*	*Amount*
1987 to 1995-96	Financial Assistance Released for DIETs	2,263.60
1995-96	Total Grant by MHRD	1,080.00

A Special Orientation Programme for Primary Teachers (SOPT) has also been taken up during the VIII Plan period. Started in late 1993, this programme is aimed at orienting an estimated 1.8 million primary teachers in the country in the use of Operation Blackboard material and MILLs strategy. The NCERT is the apex body implementing this programme through state nodal agencies which are mostly SCERTs. Ministry of Human Resource Development releases grants to the NCERT based on the needs. Within the provision of the Centrally Sponsored Scheme of Restructuring and Reorganisation of Teacher Education, so far about Rs. 450 million has been released to the NCERT for the purpose. According to the NCERT, State Governments have reported training of about 0.3 million primary teachers under the SOPT. Details on the implementation of Teacher Education Scheme have been presented earlier.

Qualifications and Training

The minimum general qualification prescribed by some states for the recruitment of primary school teachers (teaching grades I-V) is 10 years of formal education (matriculation/ secondary), whereas, it is senior secondary or 12 years of education prescribed in certain states (e.g., Haryana, Maharashtra, Tamil Nadu, Uttar Pradesh and Delhi). The minimum qualification prescribed by most states for the appointment of upper primary school teachers (teaching grades VI-VIII) is graduation (second level diploma) whereas in some states it is matriculation/senior secondary (first level diploma). The educational qualifications of teachers have been gradually increasing. According to the Fifth All India Educational Survey in 1986, as many as 2.1 million (77 per cent) primary and upper primary school teachers had been trained through first level diploma (under-graduation), 0.5 million (18 per cent) through second level diploma (graduation) and 0.1 million (5 per cent) through third level diploma (post graduation and above).

All states in India require at least a graduation degree (second level diploma) for secondary school teachers (grades VI-X and post-graduation degree (third level diploma) for higher/ senior secondary school teachers (grades XIXII). As many as 58 per cent teachers teaching at the secondary and higher secondary levels had second level diploma, 33 per cent had third level diploma and only about 9 per cent had first level diploma (under-graduation).

The above data indicates that a good percentage of teachers at all levels of school have attained the required level of general educational qualification.

Pre-service teacher Training

The Fifth All India Educational Survey indicates that about 87 per cent primary and upper primary teachers are trained, that is, they have acquired a primary or elementary teacher training certificate of one or two years' duration or bachelors degree in education. There are, however, significant regional variations. The percentage of trained teachers at primary and upper primary level is more than 99 per cent in the states of Haryana, Tamil Nadu, Chandigarh and Delhi. It is less than 50 per cent in Arunachal Pradesh, Meghalaya, Sikkim, Nagaland and Tripura.

The Centrally Sponsored Scheme of Restructuring and Reorganisation of Teacher Education taken up in 1987-88 in pursuance of NPE 1986 envisages, on the one hand, strengthening of institutional base of teacher training and on the other, takes up special programmes for training of teachers in specified areas and other non-institutional programmes of orientation for teachers. The Scheme provides for the setting up of DIETs to provide training and resource support to elementary education (both formal and non-formal) and AE systems at the grassroots level.

The scheme for establishing the DIETs envisaged raising the general education of primary teachers to 12 years of schooling. With the establishment of DIETs, almost all states are now moving towards a two-year diploma in education for those teaching at the elementary level following 12 years of schooling.

Of the total number of teachers working in high or higher secondary schools, approximately, 90 per cent are trained, i.e., they have acquired a bachelor's degree in education (B. Ed.)/, The percentage of trained teachers at both the levels is the highest in Chandigarh (99.89 and 100 per cent, respectively) and lowest in Assam (30.71 per cent and 22.52 per cent, respectively). A comparison between male and female teachers indicates that the number of male untrained teachers is more than that of female teachers at all school levels in the country.

2

Methods of Teaching

Importance of Methods and their Improvement

Need of Right Methods

Every teacher and educationist of experience knows that even the best curriculum and the most perfect syllabus remain dead unless quickened into life by the right methods of teaching and the right kind of teacher. Sometimes even an unsatisfactory and unimaginative syllabus can be made interesting and significant by the gifted teacher who does not focus his mind on the subject matter to be taught or the information to be imparted but on his students-their interests and aptitudes, their reactions and response. lie judges the success of his lesson not by the amount of matter covered but by the understanding the appreciation and the efficiency achieved by the students. In building Up, therefore, a picture of the reorganized Secondary school, it is necessary to indicate the kind of methods to be adopted and popularized if the curriculum that we have recommended is to develop into the kind of educational medium that we envisage. It is really the function of Training colleges to introduce these methods in our schools through their trained teachers and we do not propose to cover here the ground that training courses are expected to do.

Objectives of Right Methods

In discussing the problem of right methods, it is necessary to take a broad and comprehensive view of their objectives which are really closely related to the objectives of education that we have already discussed and which we must to some extent recapitulate from the point of view of methodology. A method is not merely a device adopted for communicating certain items of information to students and exclusively the concern of the teacher who is supposed to be at the "giving end." Any method, good or bad, links up the teacher and his pupils into an organic relationship with constant mutual interaction : it reacts not only on the mind of the students but on their entire personality, their standards of work and judgment, their intellectual and emotional equipment, their attitudes and values. Good methods which are psychologically and socially sound may raise the whole quality of their life ; bad methods may debase it. So, in the choice and assessment of methods, teachers must always take into consideration their end-products—namely, the attitudes and values inculcated in them consciously or unconsciously. Good methods of teaching should aim at the following objectives, which have not only intellectual but also social and moral implications, for in the domain of education, it is impossible to draw rigid lines of demarcation. Whatever impact education has on one aspect of the personality tends to react on other aspects.

The highest value that all methods should try to inculcate is love of work and the desire to do it with the highest measure of efficiency of which one is capable. There are only two real educative media, contact with a rich and well-integrated human personality and sincere, wholehearted pre-occupation with worthwhile work, intellectual as well as practical. If education fails to develop in the students a real attachment of the work that they are doing in school and the will to put the best of themselves into it, it can neither educate the mind nor train the character.

For various reasons, which we, need not analyse here, this attitude to work is not common amongst our students-either in schools or in colleges. According to our evidence they are content with the minimum of effort, Slipshod in their work, and tend to confine themselves to the study of "Notes" and "Summaries" rather than textbooks, and to textbooks rather than significant books of wider interest. The Secondary school can render no greater service to the students than by raising their standards of efficiency in every thing and creating the necessary attitude for the purpose.

The motto of every school and its pupils should be "Every thing that is worth doing at all is worth doing well"- whether it be making a speech, writing a composition, drawing a map, cleaning the classroom, making a book rack or forming a queue. From this point of view, it is more valueable to take up fewer projects and to complete them with thoroughness and efficiency than to attempt a larger number haphazardly and superficially. In this connection, it is well to remember that good work, habits, and skills are not acquired theoretically or in a vacuum; it is proper habits of work and insistance on them in every detail and over a long period of time that create the requisite attitudes and values. Discipline or cooperation. for instance, cannot be instilled into students through lectures or exhortations; they can become a part of an individual's normal technique of life only when he has been given numerous opportunities of participating in freely accepted projects and activities in which discipline and co-operation are constantly in demand for achieving the ends in view.

Another serious defect which vitiates present day teaching is its excessive domination by verbalism i.e., the tendency to identify knowledge, with words the delusion that if a student is able to memorize or repeat certain words or phrases he has grasped the facts or the ideas that they are meant to convey. The use of an imperfectly understood foreign language as medium of instruction has greatly accentuated this evil and students have usually been content, or compelled, to memorize whole paragraphs or pages from their text-books in History, Geography and even in Science and Mathematics. In spite of the change in the medium of instruction in recent years, we are afraid there has not been much improvement in this situation. The strangle-hold of verbalism is still confused with the grasp of knowledge-knowledge, which is the fruit of personal effort and purposeful intellectual and practical activity. Consequently many students leave school with a certain amount of information as their equipment but neither well-assimilated knowledge nor wisdom, which is the grace of knowledge. We felt strongly, therefore that only such methods should be adopted as will give concreteness and reality to learning and help to break down the barriers between life and learning and between the school and the community. We shall have something to say later about the nature of such methods.

On the intellectual side the most important objective of teaching methods should be to develop the capacity for clear thinking which distinguishes every truly educated person and has become increasingly important in the modern world of "plural possibilities", where every one must learn to make up his mind and judge issues and problems without prejudice or passion.

A majority of our citizens will not receive any education beyond the Secondary stage and if they cannot learn to think straight and dispassionately at this stage, they will never be able to play their part as responsible citizens of a democracy. Some of the objectives to which we have referred above will, if achieved, assist in training students in this valuable capacity. But that is not enough. It must also form the conscious objective of every single teacher, no matter what subject he is entrusted with. Whether a student is asked to make a speech in a debating society or to write an essay or to answer a question in history, geography, or science or to perform an experiment, the accent should always be on clear thinking and on lucid expression which is a mirror of clear thought.

All students cannot become eloquent speakers or good stylists but there is no reason why-if proper methods are adopted-every normal student should not be able to learn to speak and write in such a way as to convey his ideas lucidly and intelligibly. In this connection we would like to discourage the present practice of giving excessive home work. It is not only a, great burden on the children but is likely to be a threat to their health and a hindrance to the development of proper habits of work. Whatever home work is given-and we are of the opinion that this should be confined to the higher classes should be carefully and scrupulously corrected and the mistakes discussed with the students so that their confusions of thought and expression may be gradually eliminated. When a great deal of home work is given and it is not properly scrutinized by the teacher, the mistakes of spelling, of grammar, of expression of involved presentation and, above all, of confused thinking remain undetected and are likely to become ingrained. That is why a little home work, well and willingly done and carefully corrected, is far better than great deal of slipshod work reluctantly accomplished. Here as elsewhere, quality is more important than quantity. This does not of course, mean that children will do no study at home. If interest has been aroused and reading habits have been cultivated they will read many books of general interest, they will pursue their various hobbies, they may prepare charts, models diagrams or perform simple experiments and study their textbooks in various subjects. But the difference is that all this will be work, spontaneously undertaken and stemming from the students' natural interest not imposed on them from outside.

Finally, it is desirable that the methods of teaching should expand the range of students' interest. A cultured man is a person of varied interests and, if healthy interests are fostered they will enrich the personality. The normal adolescent is naturally interested in many things and in the class-room, on the playground during excursions and in their social and extra-curricular activities.

The intelligent and wide awake teacher has numerous opportunities to kindle new interest, to expand and strengthen existing ones and to satisfy their innate desire to touch life at many points. It is by exploring different avenues of interests and activities that he can truly discover himself and begin to specialize in due course. We would urge all schools to provide in the time-table at least one free period every day in which students may pursue their favourite hobbies and creative activities individually or in groups, preferably under the guidance of some interested teacher. We need hardly add that the success of this proposal would largely depend on the requisite accommodation and equipment being available for the purpose.

Value of Activity Methods

Our own observation of many schools-at-work as well as the evidence given by experienced educationists lead us irresistibly to the conclusion that the methods of teaching in use are still dominated by routine. There is still too much of cramming and the teaching in the school is not related to life, nor is there any determined attempt to check deterioration of standards of expression in speech and writing. The point of departure for all reforms in method must be the realization that knowledge has to be actively acquired by every individual student through independent effort.

The basis of teaching must therefore, be the organization of the subject matter into units or projects which would create opportunities for self-activity on the part of the students. These should largely replace the formal lessons which often lack proper motivation and, therefore, fail to arouse real interest. Students can put in their best effort only when the relationship between their life and their lessons is made manifest, for this win create the necessary feeling of interest and provide the requisite motivation.

So the business of the teacher should be to re-establish the link between life and knowledge, to share the aims and objects of teaching with his, pupils and to plan the programme of work in such a way that pupils will have varied and ample opportunities for self-expression in speech, writing, collective reading, independent research, constructive activities and other projects that bring the hand and the mind into fruitful cooperation. Such a conception of the school day programme is far removed from the stereo-typed routine of the present day in which verbalism predominates-the teacher talking and dictating notes and the children listening passively in the classroom and memorizing things at home for the sake of passing tests and examinations. There is no opportunity or desire to acquire knowledge either for the sake of life or for its own sake-the dominant motive is to scrap through the examination. If the self-activity approach is adopted, if there is imagination in planning work and freedom in its execution, the present bookish schools can be transformed into "work schools" or "activity schools" and they can become genuine centres of education for the whole personality of the child.

This approach also postulates that practical and productive work should find a prominent and honoured place in the school programme. We have already provided for it in the curriculum but what we are concerned with here is the principle that the teaching methods in all. subjects should be inspired, as far as possible, with the spirit underlying good craft work. This implies that, in the teaching of every subject opportunities should be afforded for pupils to apply practically the Knowledge that has been acquired by them.

In Geography it may take the form of drawing maps, making models, illustrations, organising excursions, keeping weather records, constructing in appropriate materials scenes from the life of different regions of the world etc. In History, in addition to the preparation of suitable illustrations of the type mentioned above, they may prepare and stage historical plays-making the costumes, the stage effects, fixing the lights etc., themselves, or cooperatively study local history, or set up a small history museum and, in fact take up any projects that will bring history to life. In connection with the study of languages—particularly the mother-tongue-they may undertake to write small booklets on subjects of special interest to them.

The collection of material from relevant sources, its editing, its actual writing, the binding of the booklets attractively-will all from part of a joyous project. Illustrated charts about great writers may be prepared-containing their pictures short notes on their life and works and brief appropriate quotations in prose or poetry from their writings-or they may possibly attempt translations of some easy books and articles in English with the object of providing rich reading material for their fellow students in the Library.

The school magazine is another project which can become the nucleus not only of creative writing but of a number of academic and practical Activities which may widen the interests and quicken the whole intellectual pace of the group of students concerned-provided, of course, it is not organised as a compulsory task imposed on the students from above but is envisaged as a creative activity initiated and directed by them spontaneously and with zest.

There is another important principle which may be borne in mind by the teacher in planning his methods of teaching. It is not the amount of knowledge imparted or learnt in class that matters but the efficiency and thoroughness with which it is acquired by the students. With the great increase in knowledge that has taken place in every single field, it is quite impossible for a student-not only in the Secondary school but even in the university-to acquire even one hundredth of the most essential knowledge in any particular field of studies. Any attempt, therefore, at an encyclopaedic approach, however watered down, is foredoomed to failure.

The teacher must concentrate on two things-quickening of interest and training in efficient techniques of learning and study. If, through proper presentation and the realisation of the relationship between the student's life and what he is learning at school, his curiosity and interest have been aroused, he will always be able to acquire necessary knowledge, on the spur of felt need. in his later life. On the other hand, the static, ready- made knowledge, which is forced on him, not only fails to irradiate his mind but is also quickly forgotten-as soon as it has been unburdened in the Examination Hall!

The emphasis therefore shifts from the quantum of knowledge to the right methods of acquiring it. For this purpose, it is essential that every student should be trained in the art of study. We consider this absolutely essential and wish to stress it in particular because, in a large majority of schools, no attempt is made to train students in this basic skill. It seems to be presumed that any one who can read a book, in the sense of passing his eyes over words or pronouncing them with his lips, has studied it. This is an untenable presumption. Study implies several mental processes-interpretation of words into their appropriate meanings, the art of building up ideas and sifting the significant from unimportant details of illustration or from incompetent "padding".

These study skills cannot be acquired automatically but have to be consciously practised. It is not necessary for us to discuss the methods that should be adopted for this purpose and for assessing whether the students have acquired the habits and capacities needed for intelligent study. But we do feel that, with reference to every subject of curriculum, the teaching of appropriate methods of study must form an important part of the school programme. One approach which has been successfully tried in some schools, is to organize, at the beginning of the session, a "How to study week" in which all the pupils concentrate on this problem are made conscious of it and are initiated into proper methods of study. But obviously this can only be useful if care is taken to see that the habits, skills and attitudes acquired during this intensive training are used throughout the year and if every teacher cooperates in this project. One essential part of this programme must be a training in the use of reference materials such as the list of contents and index in books, the dictionary, the atlas and reference books like the Encyclopaedia or the Book of Knowledge.

Adaptation of Methods to Suit Different Levels of Intelligence

Having stressed the value of activity methods, we should like also to put in Pi plea for individualized work and instruction, in order to train the students in the habit of working independently. If students are trained to do so, it will discourage cramming and make it necessary for the teacher to cover the entire course or teach the whole book through formal oral lessons. He could then concentrate on the essentials show the inter-connections of topics and arouse intelligent interest leaving some parts of the course to be studied by the students independently. There will always be certain types of assignment in the school programme which can be best carried out on the basis of individual activity. Such training is necessary not only to develop their capacity for independent work but also to adopt instruction to individual differences, these differences are a most significant part of the psychological data with which the teacher has to deal and, if he fails to adopt his methods of work and presentation to the psychological needs and mental range of different types of children, he can neither win their interest nor their active co-operation. The present practice of mechanically applying the same methods to dull average, as well as bright children is responsible for ·much of the ineffectiveness of the instruction given in schools. If these various groups of children are allowed to proceed at their own appropriate pace and the method approach as well as the curricular load are properly adjusted, it will be good for all of them-it will save the dull children from discouragement and the bright children from a sense of frustration. We commend for consideration in this connection a scheme that has been tried in schools in the United Kingdom.

The curriculum is arranged in "three streams", A, B and C. For the dull children, the curriculum as well as the syllabus in each subject are simpler and lighter-that is the C stream-and include only the minimum essential subject-matter. If they can complete that with thoroughness and efficiency they will gain more intellectually than if they were dragged behind the chariot wheels of their brighter colleagues. For the bright students the curriculum has richer content and, after they have completed the common basic contents, they can go on to study the additional subject- matter. We have not considered it necessary to work out the curriculum or the syllabuses on these lines because it will have to be done by State Departments of Education and, to some extent, by each individual school according to circumstances. But we recommend that this idea of adjusting the curriculum to students of varying ability should be explored and, what is equally important, methods of teaching should also be similarly adjusted. The brighter children will, for example, be able to respond better to methods involving greater freedom, initiative and individual responsibility than the dull or the average children who may require, at least in the early stages, a greater measure of planning and guidance by the teachers.

Balancing Individual and Group Work

A wise teacher must however, balance the claims of individual work with co-operative or group work. In actual life it is just as important to possess qualities of good tempered co-operation, discipline and leadership as to have the capacity for personal initiative and independent work. The former qualities develop best in the context of well organised group work which is not at present given its due place in our schools. The normal basis of work in a large majority of schools is competition-competition for marks and grades and prizes. This has its uses within limits but does not by any means provide the proper training for the art of living in the community. The genuine training of emotions, attitudes, and social capacities take place best in the context of projects and units of work undertaken co-operatively. It is the give- and-take of shared experiences that brings out the quality of leadership, inculcates habits of disciplined work and takes the individual out of his potentially dangerous mental and emotional isolation.

We recommend, therefore, that teachers should be so trained that they are able to visualise and organize at least a part of the curriculum in the form of projects and activity-units which groups of students may take up and carry to completion. Another advantage of such projects would be that they will break through the academic isolation of the school and bring it into vital rapport with the life and the activities of the surrounding community. The chemistry of purification of water may blossom into the study of the municipal water system; the lesson in Civics may lead to a study of the working of the Local Board or a campaign for the improvement of local sanitary conditions. In fact there are numerous resources in the life of every community which can and should, be utilised for educational purposes. Such an approach will vitalise the school and also help to improve the conditions obtaining in the community. We would like to refer in this connection to a significant educational movement that under way in the United States under the name of learning by living the object of which is to link the school and the community into a mutually enriching unity.

PLACE OF THE LIBRARY IN SCHOOLS

Need for a Proper Library Service

We have referred in an earlier part of the chapter to the importance of cultivating the habits of general reading, of reducing the stress placed on textbooks and making increasing use of the Library as repository of reference books, standard books and books of general interest. A textbook usually adopts a specific approach conveying information and knowledge as systematically and briefly as possible. Such an approach has its own advantages but it cannot provide adequate training for the growing mind of the adolescent which often craves for a wider and more challenging presentation and appreciates contact with more creative minds that textbook writers are generally gifted with.

Moreover, the standard of interest and general knowledge is so deplorably poor in Secondary schools-the examination "howlers" and the reports of Public Service Commissions are 'an irrefutable proof of the latter-that it has become a matter of the highest priority to promote the desire and the habit of general reading amongst our students. This means, in effect, the establishment of realy good libraries in schools and the provision of an intelligent and effective Library Service. In fact, without it, many of the recommendations and proposals made in this chapter and elsewhere cannot possibly be implemented. Individual work, the pursuit of group projects, many academic hobbies and co-curricular activities postulate the existence of a good, efficiently functioning library. The library may well be regarded as an essential instrument for putting progressive methods into practice. In view of its crucial importance, we consider it necessary to devote some space to discussing how the school library must be organized if it is to play its part effectively in the improvement of Secondary education. We should like to state at the out set that, in a large majority of schools there are at present no libraries worth the name.

The books are usually old, outdated, unsuitable, usually selected without reference to the students' tastes and interests. They are stocked in a few book-shelves, which are housed in an inadequate and unattractive room. The person in charge is often a clerk or an indifferent teacher who does this on a part-time basis and has neither a love for books nor knowledge of library technique. Naturally, therefore, there is nothing like an imaginative and well-planned library service which could inspire students to read and cultivate in them a sincere love of books. What makes this situation particularly difficult is the fact that most teachers and headmasters and even the educational administrators and authorities do not realize how unsatisfactory this position is and, therefore, they have no sense of urgently in matter. It is, necessary, therefore, to give some idea of the Library as we conceive it.

In the first place, the library must be made the most attractive place in the school so that students will be naturally drawn to it. It should be housed in a spacious, well-lit hall (or room), with the walls suitably coloured and the rooms decorated with flowers and artistically framed pictures and prints of famous paintings. The furniture-bookshelves, tables, chairs, reading desks-should be carefully designed with an eye to artistic effect as well as functional efficiency. As far as possible, the open shelf system should be introduced so that students may have free access to books, may learn to handle them and browse on them at their leisure. In decorating the library, the full co-operation of the students should be obtained in order to give them the feeling that it is their own library.

Secondly, the success of the library depends largely on the proper selection of books, journals and periodicals. This should be the function of a small committee of teachers who have a genuine love for books, can study book reviews, consult catalogues and visit book shops, if possible. It would be useful if the same committee could be entrusted with the work of studying children's reading interests. Both in this work as well as in the choosing of books, some senior students who are interested in reading should be associated. They are, after all, the consumers and their co-operation is likely to be very enlightening.

The guiding principle in selection should be not the teachers own idea of what books the students must read but their natural and psychological interests. If they feel more attracted, at a particular age, to stories of adventure or travel or biographies or even detection and crime, there is no justification for forcing them to read poetry or classics or belle-letters. Of course, the teacher's skill and teaching efficiency will consist in his being able to direct what they are reading now towards what they should be reading in due course. Library education postulates the gradual elevation of taste and refining of appreciation but the teachers' tact will lie in not forcing them but in unobtrusively guiding them on the way. In this endeavour, his own example and contagious enthusiasm can prove very potent allies.

The library being attractively arranged and adequately supplied with suitable books, the next important thing is an efficient service. In most schools, as we have pointed out, there is no conception of such service. It would require the services of a highly qualified and trained librarian who would be on a par with other senior teachers in pay and status and we definitely recommend that there should be, in every Secondary school, a full-time librarian of this type. If his function is merely to maintain a register of books, keep the library open at odd hours and occasionally issue books to a few students, there would obviously be no need for a full-time and highly qualified librarian. But if the library is to be the hub of the academic and intellectual life of the school, if it is not only to meet but guide the reading interests of students, if it is to work as a centre of free and supervised study as well as group. work on projects undertaken by them-if it is to do all these things, the librarian will surely have all his work cut out.

He will also be responsible for giving due publicity to good books old and new, available in the library-preparing and circulating book lists suitable for different grades, displaying blurbs and cuttings of book reviews on the notice board, arranging book exhibitions, perhaps conducting a group reading project when a few students of similar interests may come together to read aloud poems, or stories or dramas. Above all. he will be available for consultation in the selection of suitable books for general reading or references needed for individual or group projects, that they have to work out as part of their curricular or co- curricular work. It will, of course, be necessary for him to have the assistance of all his colleagues in this work-and if in the Training colleges some of them can be given a brief orientation and training in library work, it will be a great advantage-but he will have to act as the pivot and the inspiration of this intellectual and literary ferment. In this connection, it is recommended that such of those teachers as have not had any training in library work during the period of study in Training colleges should be given opportunities for attending summer courses in librarianship for periods ranging from 4 to 8 weeks.

We have recommended that every Secondary school should have a central library under a trained librarian. School buildings being what they are, it will be sometime before provision could be made in every school for a big reading room and its adjuncts. Similarly it will take time to provide each school with a qualified and trained librarian. Hence our recommendation for training some teachers in the management of school libraries as a part of their training course. These partially trained teacher-librarians will, working in cooperation gradually build up the central library and organise the library service, while in the meantime, working the class libraries. The class library is an important and essential adjunct to the central school library. It is easily organised and in the hands of a teacher of imagination it can do within its own limitations as much good work as the central library.

The important point about the class library is to change and replenish its stocks at frequent intervals so that even within the four walls of a classroom the children have a wide variety of intellectual fare spread before them. A wise class teacher can use the class library effectively to develop correct reading habits and for various other educative purposes. In a way he is in a position of advantage as compared with other teachers and if he himself loves books he is sure to infect his children with his own love and enthusiasm.

Subject Libraries

Besides the class library in every High school there should be subject libraries in charge of subject teachers. Competent subject teachers can enrich their teaching greatly with the help of small collection of books on their own subjects. These should not be confined to textbooks only. Advanced works, reference books, books on related subjects and allied fields, all these will find a place in that collection, so that handling them and browsing over them students get a wide view of the subjects in all its bearings. Nothing can be more inspiring than contact with a teacher who loves his own subject and who can present it in its proper prospective.

It is necessary for the headmasters and the teachers to keep their fingers, as it were, on the pulse of their students' general reading. At present, this is far from being the case and therefore- with the exception of the brightest students who may assume the initiative in consulting teachers about their reading-they do not receive any individual guidance in this behalf. Most teachers, in fact, have no idea of what a majority of students are reading or whether they are reading at all ! This points to the need of maintaining proper records that can be easily and quickly scrutinized. We should like to make two recommendations in this connection. Where ordinary issue registers-rather than issue cards-are maintained, each student must be allotted a few pages of the register in which all books studied by him are entered date-wise so that the class teachers and the headmaster may see at a glance what each individual has been reading and give him necessary advice and encouragement.

Secondly, each student should be required to maintain a diary in which he may enter-date-wise, the names of all the books which he has read, together with brief quotations or extracts that may appeal to him. Perhaps at a later stage, he may write short reviews or appreciations of those books. Such a diary, maintained throughout the school years, will provide a fascinating map of his intellectual development and literary growth which will not only be of value to him here and now but may be of interest even in later life.

Vacation Library and the School and the Community

We would like to make certain general suggestions in order to strengthen library facilities and to secure the maximum use of those that exist. In all public libraries there should be a section specially meant for children and adolescents which may supplement the resources of the local school libraries. Secondly, steps should be taken to keep the school library open during the vacation and long holidays for the benefit of the students as well as the local community, if possible. In places where there is no public library, the school should also consider the possibility of throwing the school library open to the public outside school hours. This may involve some extra expenditure but it would be eminently worthwhile because it will draw the school and the community into the kind of partnership that we have advocated in this Report. We are also of the view that, in States where a library cess is levied, the proceeds should also be utilised to strengthen and improve school libraries. In smaller places it may be more economical to build up the school library in such a way that it may also serve the function of a Public Library for the locality, thus avoiding the duplication of buildings and furniture, and to some extent, of staff.

In some cities we understand that during the vacation books of interest to suit different grades of students are collected from various school libraries and are placed in a central locality, the students being encouraged to visit such improvised libraries and to study whatever books they may be interested in. This is an interesting experiment that may be tried in large cities.

Need for Suitable Literature

We may, in passing, make a reference here to the associated problem of the production of suitable books for children and adolescents. At present there is a great paucity of such books in practically all Indian languages and unless the Centre and the State Governments take well thought-out measures-to encourage the production of suitable books for general reading, the objective in view cannot be realized-books suitable not only from the point of view of contents but also of printing, binding and illustrations. This may be done by giving financial assistance to qualified and well-established organizations engaged in the production of such books, by offering prizes to the best books published and by arranging translations of good children's books available in English or published in various regional languages. We believe that, if school libraries are better financed and are able to buy a larger number of books and if a love of reading is created in the students and eventually in adults with the. increased purchase of books, the law of demand and supply will come into play and more and better books will be published.

We have advocated in the preceding paragraphs several new approaches to methods of teaching and described the part a well- organized library can play in facilitating their implementation. But in the evidence and the memoranda that were tendered to us, it was repeatedly affirmed that it is very difficult to apply such progressive methods in schools. Obviously, if these ideas and suggestions are not translated into terms of curriculum and methods and the difficulties that stand in the way are not removed, Secondary education will make no headway. Some of 'these difficulties have to do with the general sense of frustration that unfortunately prevails amongst teachers.

There is no enthusiasm, no creative urge to initiate and educational renaissance. We hope, however, that soon after the publication of this Report the Central and the State Governments will undertake to organize-for the discussion of all these problems-country-wide seminars, discussion groups and refresher courses for headmasters and teachers, conducted by educationists with vision. This will help to reorient the teachers' minds and their way of thinking and create a new and bracing climate of opinion. If the improvement in the terms and conditions of service and the general social status of teachers that we have recommended elsewhere is brought about and a sense of contentment is created, we have no doubt that, as a result of these conferences, etc., the present feeling of frustration will disappear and the biggest hurdle in the way of educational reconstruction will be removed.

Role of the State in Preparing Literature

Another measure which will be very helpful in this connection is a systematic attempt on the part of all Education Departments, to prepare suitable literature, suggestive programmes, teaching aids, etc., for the guidance of teachers. At present they lack definite guidance. It is not provided by the stereotyped notes of Inspecting Officers, which can neither inspire creative thinking, nor stimulate new methods of work. The production of such material requires that there should be a small "educational wing" attached either to the office of the Director of Education or to one of the Post-Graduate Training colleges, which will devote itself exclusively to the study of educational issues and problems, with special reference to the teachers' practical difficulties, and produce pamphlets, brochures, accounts of new educational experiments and movements for their use. These should be so written that they will keep their knowledge up-to- date, introduce them to good books, inspire them to try new and better methods of teaching and give them detailed and practical suggestions for the purpose. The department should also see to it that every Secondary school has a small but select library of educational books and periodicals for the teachers' use.

Experimental Schools

Sometimes even good teachers, with ideas and a: sense of duty, are unable to put progressive educational methods into practice. Where this is not due to the uncongenial school atmosphere the reason may be either that the teachers have not been adequately trained in and given practical demonstration and observation of such methods or the pressure and dread of examination may be cramping their efforts. So far as the first reason is concerned it is a fact that even the demonstration schools attached to Training colleges often fail to put, into practice the ideas and theories advocated by the college professors. So the teachers come out of these institutions with rather vague ideas about things like 'activity methods', 'free work' and group projects etc., but they have never seen them at work. This difficulty can only be overcome if good demonstration and experimental schools are established and given all the necessary facilities, material and psychological, to develop better methods of teaching.

We should like to commend in this connection a new experiment undertaken in one of the States whereby a certain number of selected schools have been released from the usual departmental regulations about curricula, methods and textbooks and given the freedom to work on new experimental lines. If a few progressive schools are established in every State, where experienced teachers would be free to work out an improved syllabus and methods of teaching and discipline, they might, in due course, help to leave the whole educational system.

The Education Departments may also perhaps explore the possibility of short-term exchange of really gifted teachers from one school to another-particularly of teachers drawn from such progressive schools who may be sent to other institutions. So far as the system of examination is concerned, we have made recommendations elsewhere which are calculated to minimize its dead- weight and to secure greater freedom for teachers.

We recommend that such experimental schools as are in existence or which may be established in future should receive due encouragement at the hands of the State and Central Governments.

MUSEUMS AND OTHER AIDS TO EDUCATION

Museums

Museums play a great part in the education of school children as they bring home to them much more vividly than any prosaic lectures the discoveries of the past and various developments that have taken place in many fields of Science and Technology. We have seen the great value that museums play in other countries and the great importance that is attached to visits by school children at periodical intervals to these museums. They can also supply a background of information in regard to history, art and other fields of learning.

At present there are (within our knowledge) no museums in India. of the type that exist in some of the European and American cities. We believe it is necessary from the educational point of view to establish such museums in important centres at least, wherein both ancient. and modern collections will be exhibited and in some cases even demonstrations given of the actual process of development of various scientific discoveries. Nothing can impress the students in the formative age so much as the actual visualising of these experiments in graphic manner. We have seen exhibitions conducted in various museusms from time to time and have been greatly impressed with their educational value. It will serve also to educate the public at large and to give them a realistic approach to scientific investigations and scientific discoveries. It will not be difficult for every State to concentrate on one such prominent Museum at least. While on this subject we may also refer to the desirability of providing small museums in the schools themselves. It may even be possible to have a more comprehensive set-up in the museum of a particular town to which all the schools can contribute and thus make it much more attractive to school children and to the public.

We. feel that assistance from the Centre and the States should be forthcoming for the starting of such museums.

Audio-Visual Aids—Films and Radio

It is hardly necessary to emphasise the role that audio-visual aids, films and radio talks, can play in the liberalising of the education of the school children. In some States they have been developed to such an extent that most of the schools are able to obtain from the Department of Public Instruction the audio-visual aids and films and to correlate them with the particular subjects that are being taught. The students thus get not merely theoretical instruction but through these aids a graphic presentation of the subject. We recommend that a central library of educational films should be available in each State and that films of great value be sent from the Central Government to the States periodically. We recommeded also that educational films suited to Indian conditions should be taken and made available to schools.

As regards the radio, we are glad to learn that through the All- India Radio, arrangements have been made for school broadcasts. It is hardly necessary for us to emphasise that such broadcasts should be by well-qualified persons and should create an interest in the subject so that the boy's curiosity can be roused to learn more about the subject. Nothing is calculated to produce in the child an aversion for such broadcasts as the monotonous and none too graphic description that sometimes is given by persons not quite familiar with the psychology of the young mind. It should not be treated as a routine duty which can be discharged by any teacher in the area. Care must be taken to see that an expert panel of headmasters and teachers is constituted to decide on (a) the subject to be dealt with, (b) the manner in which it ought to be dealt with, and (c) persons competent to give such a talk. If school broadcasts are to be conducted on these lines, they will form a very efficient supplement to education.

We venture to hope that the adoption of the various suggestions that have been made as well as the practical measures that have been recommended will break through the vicious circle which holds our schools in its thrall and release forces which will eventually transform the educational system.

Improvement of the Teaching Personnel

The Need for Improving the General Conditions of Teachers

In the preceding chapters of our Report we have referred to the various steps to be taken to improve the quality and standards of Secondary education and to make it a worthy medium for the balanced development of the students' personality. We are, however, convinced that the most important factor in the contemplated educational reconstruction is the teacher-his personal qualities, his educational qualifications, his professional training and the place that he occupies in the school as well as in the community.

The reputation of a school and its influence on the life of the community invariably depend on the kind of teachers working in it. Priority of consideration must, therefore, be given to the various problems connected with the improvement of their status. During our tour, we were painfully impressed by the fact that the social status, the salaries and the general service conditions of teachers are far from satisfactory.

In fact, our general impression is that on the whole their position today is even worse than it was in the past. It compares unfavourably not only with persons of similar qualifications in other professions but also, in many cases, with those of lower qualifications who are entrusted with less important and socially less significant duties. They have often no security of tenure and their treatment by management is in many cases, inconsistent with their position and dignity.

The same story of woe was repeated at almost every centre by the Teachers' Organizations and by responsible headmasters and others interested in education. It is surprising that, in spite of the recommendations made by successive Education Commissions in the past many of the disabilities from which teachers suffer, still persist and adequate steps have not been taken to remove them. We are aware that in recent years, in many States, there has been a revision of teachers' grades and dearness allowances' have been sanctioned. But they have not brought adequate relief, be-' cause, meanwhile, the cost of living has risen steeply and thus nullified the concessions that had been granted. We are fully conscious of the financial difficulties of the State Governments and the fact that they have to attend simultaneously to a large number of urgent and pressing problems. But we are convinced that, if the teachers' present mood of discontent and frustration is to be removed and education is to be. come a genuine nation-building activity, it is absolutely necessary to improve their status and their conditions of service.

Method of Recruitment

There seems to be no uniform system in the different States in regard to the recruitment of teachers. We have referred elsewhere to the measures that may be adopted to attract the best persons to the profession by giving them stipends and treating them as on probation during the period of training. Many schools have still a large number of untrained teachers and it does not seem to have been realised by managements that it is unfair on their part to let the students be taught by such teachers.

Some management's utilise untrained teachers for short periods and then discharge them and thus circumvent the departmental rules regarding the employment of trained teachers. We realise that the training facilities available are not adequate and that a considerable increase in the number of training institutes is necessary. Still we are not convinced that the managements have taken all the steps possible to attract trained teachers. We feel that there should be a reasonably uniform procedure for the selection and appointment of teachers and this should not be very different as between Government schools and schools under the management of private agencies. In the case of Government schools, the Public Service CommisSion selects teachers-at least in the higher grades-and in doing so they have the advice of the Director of Education or some other high official of the Department. In privately managed schools, however, the procedure varies from State to State and sometimes from institution to institution. We recommend that in all privately managed institutions there should be a small Selection Committee. entrusted with the responsibility of recruiting the staff, with the headmaster as an ex-officio member. It is also desirable that a nominee of the Department of Education should be on the Managing Board. We also recommend that, in schools maintained by local boards or municipalities, a similar policy should be adopted and either the Public Service Commission of the State or a body constituted on similar lines should be entrusted with the task of selecting teachers.

Period of Probation

At present there is no uniformity in regard to the period of probation prescribed for teachers. Unless it is short-term vacancy, it is desirable that a trained teacher, appointed to a permanent post, should be on probation for one year, and after satisfactory completion of the period he should be confirmed. In exceptional cases, the managements may extend that period by one year which should be the maximum period of probation before deciding confirmation. After confirmation, the teacher should normally be continued in service till the age of retirement.

Qualifications of Teachers in High and Higher Secondary Schools

We have already stated that, so far as the High schools are concerned only graduates with a degree in education should be appointed. We feel that at the Middle school stage also it is important to have a fair number of trained graduates on the staff. It is our hope that, in course of time, education at the Middle school stage win be imparted by graduate teachers, and Secondary grades trained teachers will be available for Primary or Junior Basic schools. We recommend this for consideration as a long-term plan.

In regard to the appointment of teachers for technical and technological subjects included in the diversified courses of study, the qualification should be prescribed by the departments of education after taking into consideration the requirements of the particular subject to be taught. In the majority of cases, we recommend that such teachers should be graduates in the particular subject and should have received training in teaching it.

We have noted that at present, in many schools, the staff appointed satisfy only the minimum educational qualifications prescribed. It is very desirable that at least some of the teachers should possess higher educational qualifications both in general education and in teaching.

Many universities have given teachers employed in recognised schools the privilege of taking the examination for a higher degree after private study. As an incentive for the acquisition of such additional qualifications, we suggest that school authorities should grant some additional increments to teachers who obtain higher degrees while in service. Care must, however, be taken to see that this does not interfere with the satisfactory discharge of their normal duties.

We have recommended that the Secondary school course should be extended to cover an additional year and that at the end of this period candidates must be eligible for the Higher Secondary schools certificate. This additional year of school course carries with it the responsibility for greater efficiency in teaching and for the attainment of a higher standard. It is necessary before any school is recognised as Higher Secondary school that teachers with higher qualifications should be appointed to the staff. We found that in one State, whenever a school is upgraded into a Higher Secondary school, it was incumbent upon the management to have on the staff persons with higher qualifications the number of such teachers depending upon the number of subjects taught in the school. In view of the fact that one year of the old Intermediate is to be added to the Higher Secondary schools, we feel that the qualifications of the teachers entrusted with the last two years at the Higher Secondary stage should be the same as prescribed in some universities for teachers of the Intermediate.

These qualifications are the Honours or M.A. Degree or a first Class B.A. with a degree in teaching. For the traditional period we suggest that persons employed in Higher Secondary schools should have these high academic qualifications and possess either a degree in Education or at least three years' teaching experience in a college. In the Higher Secondary schools which impart instruction in the technical and vocational sub- jects some of the teachers dealing with the last two years should likewise possess high qualifications in their own subjects. These may be prescribed by the special advisory committees which we have suggested for technical education.

We have referred in another chapter to the importance of properly trained teachers of languages at the school stage. If, as we envisage, students have to be taught two or more languages, the need for properly trained teachers becomes even greater. At present, in a number of schools, the language teacher is required to have a university qualification and in some State qualifications awarded by certain other bodies have been recognised as equipment. We trust this recognition has been given with due reference to their academic standards, and that government have satisfied themselves about the courses, the methods of teaching and qualifications of staff. We feel that unless this is done, there will be wide variation in the standard of attainment of language teacher in different schools. These teachers, like the teachers of other subjects, require special training in method of teaching. In some States such training is provided for language teachers and certificates are awarded by the University or the Government. We recommend that all other States should likewise arrange for the training of graduates, oriental title holders and other persons possessing necessary linguistic qualifications.

Conditions of Service

In addition to what we have stated above there are certain other important conditions of service which merit consideration.

(a) *Scale of pay:* Considerable dissatisfaction exists everywhere about the scales of pay for teachers in the different grades of schools. Certain minimum scales of pay have been recommended by successive committees and commissions as well as in the Reports of the Central Pay Commission, the Central Advisory Board of Education and the Kher Committee. These recommendations, have not, however, been implemented and as we have pointed out, the concessions actually made have been largely nullified by the phenomenal increase in the cost of living. The problem therefore requires urgent consideration.

Apart from the question of the actual scales of pay sanctioned we see no justification for variations in the grades of teachers working in government schools and in schools conducted by local bodies and private agencies in the same State. We recommend as a general principle that those who have similar qualifications and undertake similar responsibilities should be treated on a par in the matter of salary irrespective of the type of institution in which they are working. We have noted that in some States the scales of pay are much lower than on other States. We wish to emphasise that the revision of the present scales of pay is urgent and this revision should take into due consideration the recommendations made by previous committees during the last few years as well as the increase in cost of living that has occurred since then. Since the cost of living as well as the financial position of different States vary considerably, it is not possible for us to suggest a uniform pay scale applicable in all States. We, therefore, strongly urge that the States should appoint special committees to review the scales of pay of teachers of all grades and make recommendations that meet in a fair and just manner, the present cost of living.

(b) *Provident funds and pension:* Apart from the scales of salary the general conditions of service should be such that teachers can duly discharge their family and civic responsibilities without anxiety about their future and the security of service. At present they are entitled to Provident Fund benefits in most of the States. The contribution made to the Fund by the teachers, the States and private managements vary considerably. Generally, the teacher subscribes an amount not exceeding 6 1/4 % of his salary and an equal amount is contributed by the management and the State or by the Local Board concerned, the whole amount being invested in some kind 'of securities and paid to him at the end of his service. Teachers who are transferred from one educational institution to another have the right to have their Provident Fund also transferred. In some States, however, an equal contribution is not made to the Provident Fund by the parties concerned.

Teachers in government service are entitled to pension as in other services of government but not so the teachers in private schools. We have had several unfortunate cases where the sudden demise of a teacher has left the family almost penniless and the Provident Fund did not meet even the immediate needs of the family. It is, therefore, necessary to think of other ways of overcoming such difficulties.

Triple Benefit Scheme for Teachers

Recently, in one of the States, a triple benefit scheme has been instituted for government servants, called the Pension-cum-Provident Fund-cum-Insurance Scheme. We understand that this scheme has been introduced by some universities also for their employees. We feel that, if the teachers are to be relieved of worries about the future of their family, this triple benefit scheme should be made applicable to teachers in all States.

Security of Tenure

The teaching profession in the country is much perturbed, about security of tenure of office and the general conditions under which they have to work. In some States, schools have been established by managements who have no experience of educational work. There is no doubt that many managements have abused their position and treated teachers shabbily and this is probably responsible for the demand by some teachers and Teachers' Associations that all schools should be brought under the control of the government. We have also received complaints that service conditions under local bodies have been unsatisfactory and that teachers have been subjected to humiliating treatment by the authorities concerned in the matter of transfer, termination of services, and punishments. In brief the present position of these bodies and their relationship to the teaching profession is not satisfactory. We have been told by responsible teachers and Teachers' Associations that it is not unusual for some managements to ask for "voluntary donations" from the teachers for the schools. We consider it essential that all those who have to do with educational administration should recognise clearly and without any mental reservation the status of the teachers and the respect and consideration due to them. At the same time we must strongly affirm that it is the duty of teachers to set up such a high example of personal and professional integrity as to win the respect as well as the full co-operation of the management and the community.

It has also been brought to out notice that punishment are sometimes meted out to teachers inconsiderately-their services are terminated or their transfers made without adequate grounds or increments stopped without justification. While we would not suggest that an erring teacher should not incur any punishment, we feel that whenever such punishment are meted out there should be provision for an appeal by the teacher to a higher authority. We are aware that, in certain States, the managements are required to report to the Director of Public Instruction certain types of disciplinary action. For this purpose, Arbitration Boards or Committees should be appointed which will have a right to look into these appeals and any grievances and to consider whether the punishment accorded, suspension, dismissal, stoppage of increments, or reduction to a lower status is justified. This board should consist of the Director of Education or his nominee, a representative of the management and representative of the State Teachers' Association. The decision of the Board should be final, except in the case of government servants who have the right to, appeal to a higher authority i.e., government. Where a local board has a number of schools under its management, we deem it desirable that there should be a special officer of the Education Department to look after the conditions of service of teachers employed under it. In the case of girls' schools the special officer should be a woman of the status of an Inspectress of Schools. These officers should be authorised to deal with transfers, appointment, etc.. subject to a right of appeal either to the Director of Education or the Arbitration Board according to the nature of the case.

Age of Retirement

At present, the age of retirement is 55, but in private institutions, it can be extended up to 60 with the approval of the Department of Education. We. feel that in view of the expanding need for qualified teachers and in view also of the improvement in the general expectation of life within recent years, the age of retirement may be extended to 60 with the approval of the Director of Education provided the teacher is physically and otherwise fit.

Other Amenities

In addition to the above specific recommendations we feel that there are certain other amenities that should be provided for the teaching profession so as to attract the right type of persons. Among these may be mentioned the following:

(i) *Free education of children:* Free education up to the age of 14 is a responsibility of government under the Constitution. It would therefore, be in keeping with this policy, if the children of teachers are given free education in schools. We were glad to note that in one State the children of all the teachers are given free education up to the middle school stage, and half-fee concession at the high school stage, the State compensating the managements concerned for the loss of fee on this account. We recommend this policy and suggest that the children of teachers should be given free education throughout the school stage.

(ii) *Housing schemes for teachers:* One of the difficulties experienced in recruiting teachers both for urban and rural areas is the lack of suitable accommodation. This difficulty is even greater in the case of women teachers, and instances have come to our notice of women teachers transferred to certain places being entirely unable to find any residential accommodation at all. We suggest that through a system of co-operative house-building societies or in other ways teachers should be provided with quarters so as to enable them to live near the schools and devote more of their time to the many sided activities of the School.

(iii) *Railway travel concessions:* Teachers have to attend seminars and refresher courses organised by the Department of Education or by Teachers' Associations, and they should be encouraged to attend regional and All-India Educational Conferences. We were told that the railway authorities have extended certain travel concessions to them. We welcome this move and, recommend that it should be widened so that teacher wishing to go to health resorts or holiday camps or to attend educational conferences, seminars, etc., be given travel concessions at half rates.

(iv) *Holiday homes and health resorts:* One of the teachers' special advantages is the long vacation during which they are expected to refresh themselves both in body and mind and 'equip themselves better for their work when the school reopens. It would be of advantage to start a nation-wide movement encouraging teachers to go to health resorts or holiday homes during the vacation. This should not be very difficult or costly, if managements and State Governments co-operate to organise such, camps on a permanent basis and afford necessary facilities to teachers to spend at least part of their vacations in such camps. In some States a beginning has been made in this direction, and we would like to commend this example to other States and private managements.

(v) *Medical relief:* We feel that the teaching profession should be entitled to the benefit to medical relief, free treatment in hospitals and dispensaries, and, where necessary, free accommodation in State hospitals. We were glad to learn that in one of the States, all non-gazetted officers were entitled to this concession. The extension of this privilege to the teaching profession as a whole will be greatly appreciated and will go a long way to relieve them of anxiety.

(vi) *Leave concessions:* We have stated elsewhere that the minimum number of working days in a school should be about 200. In a large majority of cases, the teacher will get the benefit of the vacation and the other causal holidays. Under certain circumstances, however, special leave may be necessary on account of illness or urgent personal work. There are three types of leave, which may be considered in this connection—causal leave, medical leave, and, in the case of women teachers, maternity leave We recommend that there should be uniform leave rule for all educational institutions.

In addition to the kinds of leave mentioned above there is a great deal to be said in favour of study leave being granted to teachers. Opportunities must be given to them to visit different institutions within the country and some of them, in responsible position, may be given study leave on full pay to go abroad, for period ranging from 6 months to 12 months, for higher education or to study educational work in foreign countries. Such study leave should be granted by the Centre or the State Government concerned, and the teachers selected may be either from Government or Local Boards or Private schools, the chief criterion for selection being the extent to which he will gain by his study and experiences for use on his return. Study leave may also be granted to obtain higher qualifications in teaching or any other relevant subject of study.

The system of granting a "subbatical year's leave" that exists in some countries of the West may also be considered with advantage by the State and Central Governments.

Problem of Additional Employment

The most usual form of remunerative work taken up by the teachers out of school hours consists of private tuitions. This practice of private tuitions has unfortunately assumed the proportions of an educational scandal. We are satisfied that it is attended with several evils. Steps should be taken to abolish it as early as possible. In view of the recommendations we have made for the improvement of the conditions of service. we believe it will become increasingly unnecessary for teachers to take up private tuitions to supplement their income. We are aware that some students require special coaching to keep pace with other children but the right way of dealing with that situation is that the school should itself make provision for extra tuition to such backward children at fixed hours charging extra fees for purpose if necessary.

We do not wish, to make any definite recommendations in this matter but would leave to the State to consider whether, consistently with their school duties, some of the teachers in the rural areas could not be utilised for other local duties like Post Office or Rural Reconstruction 'Work such as being carried on by the Community Projects on a remunerative basis. In view of the paucity of educated persons in rural areas this kind of part-time employment may enable the teacher to perform some useful work for the local community and earn some additional income.

Teachers' Status in Society

We have already referred to the importance of the teachers' social status. There is a growing feeling, that the lead in this matter should be taken by persons in high public positions who should show special recognition of the status and dignity of teachers and treat them not on the basis of their salary and economic status but on the importance of the nation-building work that is entrusted to them. If they do so, society would follow their example in due course. At important public and ceremonial functions, the head of the State or the Ministers or the District Officer concerned should invite representatives of the teaching profession and give them a position of honour. Many in the profession have shown outstanding merit in their work and are entitled to receive due recognition of it from the State as well as from the society. They must also be consulted in all important matters pertaining to education so as to strengthen their sense of professional responsibility.

Headmaster

Special mention must be made of the position of the headmaster in a school. On him the proper working of the school ultimately depends. The reputation of a school and the position that it holds in the society depends in a large measure on the influence that he exercises over his colleagues, the pupils and their parents and the general public. Similarly the dicipline of the school and its esprit de crops are his special responsibility. He also holds an important place in the life of the community, where he can exercise a very healthy influence. By this contact with parents and the general public he can help to forge that link between the school and the larger community which we have repeatedly stressed. He is also responsible for carrying out the policies and programme of the Department of Education and he acts a liaison between it and the management or the general local community.

From all these points of view the choice of the headmaster of the school is of particular significance. By his attainments and qualifications, his previous record as a teacher, his social aptitudes, he should be able to command the confidence of his colleagues and the public and the respect of his pupils. We believe that seniority is frequently not the best criterion in the choosing of a headmaster. It is more important that he should possess the other conditions and qualifications that we have mentioned as necessary for such a high and responsible post.

The special qualifications to be stressed in addition to the academic and professional are teaching and/or administrative experience of at least 10 years and qualities of leadership and administrative ability.

We belive that to attract people of the right type to so responsible a position, the emoluments of the post should be sufficiently attractive. For this purpose a special scale of pay or an allowance in addition to this salary should be given. To enable him to discharge his duties efficiently the number of students in the school must be limited. We have stated elsewhere that the optimum number in a school is 500 and the maximum 750 except in certain multipurpose schools where it may be 1,000 and where the headmaster should have a Deputy to look after vocational side or the general side as the case may be. Where the number exceeds this limit, a senior teacher should be designated as Assistant Headmaster and certain duties of the headmaster should be delegated to him. It is of the utmost importance however that headmaster should have opportunities of getting into contact with all the pupils in the school, to scrutinize their records, to get to know the parents and to participate in the co-curricular and the community activities of the school.

In conclusion, we should like to reiterate that the whole question of educational reconstruction hinges on the success the Department and the community in winning over the whole hearted co- operation of the teachers. For this purpose, the necessary climate of opinion must be created. This should be done not only through the various measures that we have recommended for improving their economic and social status but also by organizing nation-wide conferences, study groups, discussions and seminars at which creative ideas about educational reform may be discussed and popularized.

TEACHER-TRAINING

Importance of Training of Teachers

Having considered the general question relating to the improvement of the teachers' status it is necessary to devote special attention to the problems of their training. It has been noted that there are considerable variations in regard to the teacher-training programme in different States and also that the number of institutions for teacher-training is very inadequate compared even to the present needs. Moreover, the prospects of teaching profession are not satisfactory enough to attract sufficient number of candidates to join the teacher-training institutions.

Types of Teacher-Training Institutions

Broadly speaking, the existing teacher-training institutions may be classified under three heads:

(i) Primary (or Basic) Teacher-Training;

(ii) Secondary Teacher-Training; and

(iii) Graduate Teacher-Training Institutions.

The Primary (or Basic) Teacher-Training Institutions are inten- ded for teachers of Primary or junior Basic schools. The general educational qualification of these teachers varies from State to State, but on the whole it is not high. In some States they should have read up to the third form or the eighth standard of the High School or they should have completed the Higher Elementary course. Thereafter they are given one or two years' training and are then expected to teach in Elementary or primary or junior Basic schools as they may be variously called.

Need for Better-Equipped Teaching Personnel

It is an accepted principle that teaching in the lower standards and especially in infant classes in the Primary grades requires as much, if not more, preparation as in the High schools and that the lower the grade of pupils the greater is the skill required to teach them. In the course of our tour, we have observed with pleasure in some nursery schools and primary schools conducted by private agencies to what extent the quality of teaching improves when educated and well-trained persons are in charge. We have seen how the boys and girls in these schools are not merely given training in the three 'R's' but are also trained in habits of life and social conduct and in some elementary craft work which helps in the development of personality and creates in children a healthy interest in and a love for education.

These principles are no doubt implemented in what is known as the Basic typo of education. The point to be emphasised is that proper education at this very early stage is not possible with the type of teachers as are now accepted for Primary schools. If a good foundation is to be laid at this most impressionable stage, efforts should be made to see that better equipped and better trained teachers are available. We are, therefore, of the opinion that the minimum general educational standard for all Primary school teachers should be the School Leaving Certificate and that their period of training should extend over two years and it should consist of training both in general as well as in the professional subjects.

In our opinion, there should be only two types of institutions for teacher-training: (1) for those who have taken the School Leaving Certificate or the Higher Secondary School Leaving Certificate as envisaged by us, and for whom a two-year teacher-training should be required; and (2) for graduates for whom the training should be, as at present, of one academic year. We suggest as a long-term programme that graduate teachers should have their training extended to two academic years; but we realise that both financially and in view of the number of teachers required and also because the teachers them- selves can ill spare two years for such training, this is not immediately possible.

Graduate or First-Grade Teacher-Training

In regard to graduate teacher-training, we are definitely of the opinion that institutions for this purpose should be recognised by and affiliated to the universities and the diplomas and degrees should be granted by the universities and not by the State Departments of Education or by ad hoc bodies. In some States, it would appear that some graduate teachers obtain as their training qualification a degree awarded by a university while others obtain for the same purpose a diploma given by the State Department of Education. We consider that the maintenance of two standards in training is wholly unnecessary. It is not desirable that the State through their Departments of Education should conduct tests and grant diplomas at this stage. Graduate training being a post-graduate qualification should come under the university and when there are universities carrying on this function, all graduates should be trained in institutions which are affiliated to the universities and submit to tests conducted by the university. As for the other type of teacher-training institutions, they should be under the control of a separate Board appointed for this purpose and not under the Department of Education. We shall refer to the constitution and functions of such a

Board later. In some States even these are under the control of the university; but we do not think that the university can effectively supervise and guide the large number of such institutions catering for many thousands of teachers.

Secondary-Grade Training

In the secondary-grade training institutions for which we have recommeded a two-year course, the first year will be devoted largely to general education. The student-teachers' interest in teaching should be stimulated by visits to schools, discussions and some amount of teaching practice under supervision. In the second year, special subjects pertaining to pedagogy and the practice of methods of teaching should form a large part of the curriculum. Secondary-grade trained teachers should largely be employed for the nursery schools and the primary or junior Basic schools. While every one of them may probably be given training to deal with general subjects in these different types of schools, some should have special training in one or other of the following :

(a) Nursery-school education.

(b) Craft education and principles of craft-centred education.

(c) One or other of co-curricular activities.

The general approach to co-curricular activities will be taught to all, but one or two of these co-curricular activities should be more intensively taken up by the student-teachers for a limited period of training, say for 8 or 12 weeks. The object of the special training in such co-curricular activities like physical education, scouting and guiding, first-aid, excursion, library organisations etc., is to provide teachers specially trained to organise these activities properly.

Graduate-Training

Graduate-training is restricted to one year, and although we have recommended as a long-term programme the desirability of increasing this period to two academic years, we realise that it cannot be thought of in the immediate future. During this one year of training, the graduate teacher should be trained in methods of teaching at least two subjects. The subjects so chosen should have studied, at least up to the .Intermediate or Higher Secondary Certificate standard. This point is important. For we are told that in many instances graduates with a combination of subjects which have nothing to do with schools come for training. Such graduates, even with training, can hardly make good subject-teachers. They should, therefore, be discouraged from joining the teaching profession.

Practical Training

The importance to be attached to teaching practice in schools cannot be over-emphasised. We believe that it will be conducive to sound training if every Teacher-Training college has a demonstration school-more commonly called a model school-as well as a certain number of other schools at a reasonably near distance associated with it for purposes of practical training. These schools themselves should have trained graduate teachers on the staff. We do not propose to enter into the details with regard to the nature of the training that is to be imparted but we wish to emphasise that at present the practical training for student-teachers is very limited and in some places almost non-existent. There is one point, however, which should be mentioned in this connection. The practical training should not consist only of practice in teaching, observation, demonstration and criticism of lessons, but should include such subjects as construction and administration of scholastic tests, Organisation of supervised study and students' societies, conducting library periods and maintenance of cumulative records. We feel that the scope of teacher training, particularly in its practical aspects, should be broadened to include some of these activities that a student-teacher will be expected to perform when he becomes a full fledged teacher.

One aspect of such specialised training deserves attention. The training of teachers of handicapped children concerns not only the physically handicapped but also the mentally handicapped children. Teachers of mentally handicapped children also need very special kind of training in which problem of mental disorders and mental hygiene should figure prominently. It would however, be an advantage if A teachers are initiated during their training into the general principles of mental hygiene because of the insight it provides into the behaviour problems of even ordinary children. In fact we are of opinion that mental hygiene should receive greater emphasis than it at present does in the teacher training courses at all levels.

As regards the assessment of a teacher's practical ability, we realise that it is not possible for large numbers to have an examination test in practical training conducted by an outside agency like the university, but internal tests by the staff should be required in all cases, supplemented where necessary by sample test by the Board of Examiners conducting the university examination.

Training in Co-Curricular Activities

In view of the importance we attach to co-curricular activities, to which reference has been made elsewhere, every student-teacher should have special training in one or other of the co-curricular activities in a manner we have suggested for secondary-grade trained teachers. The object of this training is not to supplant the fully trained personnel, but rather to supplement their activities and to give them valuable assistance in this respect.

Thus, a short course of training in school librarianship will enable the teacher concerned to give valuable assistance to the trained librarian of the school. Likewise, training in physical education will enable the teacher to co-operate with the medical officer, and with the physical education teachers in looking after the physical welfare of the school children. So far as medical care is concerned, we have in another place referred to the fact that student teachers can be given a short period of training in regard to certain fundamentals of school health and care of the children; we have also stated that school teachers so trained would form a useful link with the other trained staff in looking after the health and welfare of the school children. Each training institution must develop along these lines so as to supplement the usual teacher-training programme by intensive courses over short periods for teachers With particular aptitudes in any of the co- curricular activities. Likewise, training in school administration, audio-visual education, school broad-casts, social education, scouting and guiding, citizenship, training, junior Red Cross as well as training in conducting students' clubs, debating societies, etc. and in organising social service and community life can be given to the student-teachers. Many of these activities require a good deal of knowing and preparation if they are to be effectively utilised in the school programme.

In-Service Training

However excellent the programme of teacher-training may be, it does not by itself produce an excellent teacher. It can only engender the knowledge skills and attitudes which will enable the teacher to begin his task with a reasonable degree of confidence and with the minimum amount of experience. Increased efficiency will come through experience critically analysed and through individual and group efforts at improvement. The teacher training institution should accept its responsibility for assisting in this in-service stage of teacher-training. Among the activities which the training college should provide or in which it should collaborate are : (1) refresher courses, (2) short intensive courses in special subjects, (3) practical training in workshop, (4) seminars and professional conferences. It should also allow its staff where possible to serve as consultants to a school or group of schools conducting some programme of improvement.

Liasion Between Training Institutions and Other Agencies

Training institutions should be in close liaison with the Department of Education and the schools. Such close relationship will be fruitful in many ways specially in regard to the placing of student-teachers. Except in the case of deputed teachers, training institutions are not now in a position to do anything for placing other students in educational institutions. It would be to the advantage of all concerned if training institutions could keep in touch with their alumni and follow their subsequent careers. In recruiting teachers, therefore, training colleges should be consulted by the department as well as by the other agencies.

Training Colleges and Research in Education

One aspect of the training college should not be lost sight of. The training college should in essence be not merely a college for training teachers, but an institution for research work in all aspects of pedagogy.

The staff of the college should be such as would be capable of devoting some of their time to research in curricular and extra- curricular activities, general administration, modern trends of pedagogy and also from time to time in research to evaluate results of the particular method of training adopted in different schools. For this purpose every training college desiring to conduct educational research should have under its control an experimental or demonstration school besides the practising schools already mentioned.

Training in Special Subjects

There are certain special types of training which are being given in different institutions. Physical education, for instance, is at present given in specialised institutions for the purpose. Likewise, training for handicapped children, for deaf-mutes and the blind are given in separate institutions. Rightly so, for the effectiveness of the training will be preserved only if given in institutions where the. principles of pedagogy in relation to these particular subjects concerned will be given due emphasis.

Recruitment to Training Colleges

Recruitment to training colleges should be carefully made so as to admit only those who hold the highest promise of becoming successful teachers. Admission. should generally be carefully devised after tests and interviews. We cannot afford to waste money on training people who have not the making of good teachers. We have had enough evidence to show that in many places it has not been possible to recruit a sufficient number of trainees to meet the needs of the schools in the State. Even where a sufficient number of recruits is available, they seldom possess high qualifications. This is no doubt owing to the present very unsatisfactory position of teachers' status and emoluments. As long as the conditions of service and salary are so unattractive and the status of teachers remains low and unimportant corn. pared with other learned professions, there is no possibility of drawing large numbers of really qualified, enthusiastic and devoted candidates to join the profession. We have referred elsewhere to the Urgent need of improving the conditions of teachers in all these respects.

There is one other aspect of the question, however, which we wish, to emphasise at this stage. There is great diversity in regard to the terms offered to student-teachers in the different training institutions in the States. In some institutions the training is given free; in other a fee is charged. Taking into consideration the need for a very large number of teachers and also the need for attracting the right type of teachers to the profession, we recommend that no fees should be charged in training colleges and all student- teachers should be given suitable stipends by the State during the period of training. This was the practice some years ago. We also suggest that teachers already in service should be given, during the period of training the same salary which they were getting. They should, however, under such circumstances, be expected to execute a bond to serve as teachers for a period of five years. This will apply both to graduate teachers and to second-grade teachers.

We have suggested that young pupils who show promise of developing into good teachers should be recruited. We wish to point out that the teachers themselves are potentially recruiting agents par excellence. By their attitude towards the public and the students, they are daily recruiting young people into or out of the profession. At the upper secondary school level and in the undergraduate colleges, teachers can perform an outstanding service to students and the profession if they actively encourage young people who possess intelligence and other characteristics which may lead to success in teaching, to consider teaching as their career. Such students, after graduation, may serve for some period in some school and acquire practical experience before going in for professional training.

Preparation of Teachers Before Admission and Duration of Course

In view of the comparatively short duration of the training course at present, it is suggested that the selection of the students for teacher training may be made some months in advance of the opening of the course. The majority of candidates will be those who are already teaching or who have settled on teaching as their profession. During this period, they may be given opportunities to study some selected books recommended by the training colleges concerned, so that when they come for training they will have some information as a back- ground for the study they are to launch upon. We suggest that the period of training may be increased to a minimum of 180 days by eliminating the number of unnecessary holidays. Within this period, it should be possible for the students to have practical training in schools and to have the theoretical training in the subjects concerned and some training in a few of the co-curricular activities.

Residential Training Colleges

There is one aspect of the life of the student-teacher which we wish to emphasise. We believe that the time at the disposal of the student-teacher, whether in the second-grade or the graduate-grade, is so limited that his whole time should be devoted to the study of various aspects of education, school life, community life, administration, etc.

Life in the training institutions should be a guide to the activities in the school with the pupils. We wish, therefore, to emphasise that this community life in the training institutions, the devotion to the various activities that can be attempted in such institutions and the mixing of the student-teacher themselves in all social and useful activities both in the school community as well as in the community life of the area where the school is situated would best be promoted by a residential system of training. We, therefore, strongly advocate a residential type of training institutions for all students. Such residence will train them in self-reliance, provide a certain amount of manual labour and cultivate community life within and outside the school premises. We expect them to manage their own hostels, to take turns in the different kinds of work connected with the kitchen and the dining room, to be responsible for the general cleanliness of the institution, and thus to develop habits of healthy and active living and sense of the dignity of labour.

Post-Graduate Course in Education

We have referred to research in training institutions. This brings up to post-graduate training in Education. We feel that there is scope for post-graduate courses in Education and we are glad to note that in some of the universities a post-graduate degree, the Master of Education, has been instituted. A clearer conception of what is intended by the Master's degree in education seems to us to be required. This degree is primarily intended for higher studies in pedagogy: (1) to give ideas through the study of comparative education of modern methods that are being followed in different countries, (2) to, cultivate aptitude for research so that experiments on new methods and techniques of education suited to the country and the community may be undertaken, (3) to afford opportunities for specialisation in one or other of the branches of study pertaining to (a) the curricula of school studies, (b) craft-centred education, (c) co-curricular activities, etc., and (4) to train teachers for higher grades in the profession such as the headmaster, the inspectorate, and teaching staff of training institutions. In fact this higher education should be designed to inculcate the qualities of leadership in education.

At present the Master's degree can be taken immediately after the first degree in education. Owing to the limited number of seats the selection is more often made from those who have had experience as teachers subsequent to their first degree in teaching, but it is not limited. to such people. We believe that it would be an advantage if for this higher degree in education trained teachers who have done normally a minimum of three years teaching in a school are only selected. It is desirable that a certain number of scholarships should be made available for such teachers for the period of study they have to put in for the higher degree and that the teachers concerned may be selected after consideration of their qualifications, their record as school teachers, their aptitude for research shown by any contributions that they may have made, their general personality and their conduct in the profession.

Staff of Training Colleges

From what has been stated above, it seems obvious that care should be taken in selecting the staffs of training colleges whether for the second grade institutions or the first i.e., graduate training colleges. We believe that there should be a picked staff of teachers possessing (i) a good general educational qualification; (ii) a degree in teaching; and (iii) at least five years of experience as a teacher in a school. An additional qualification may be three to five years experience as an Inspector.

In the case of second grade training institutions the minimum qualification should be a first or second class bachelor's degree, with an L. T. or B. T. qualification. In the case of graduate training institutions, the minimum qualification should be (i) an Honours or Master's degree, or a, first class B.A. or B.Sc. degree in the particular subject, (ii) a. professional qualification a Master of Education degree with three years' teaching experience or an L. T. or B. T. degree with five years' service as an Inspector or headmaster. We are of opinion that there should be a free exchange between professors in training colleges on the one hand and selected headmasters of schools and Inspectors of the Education Department on the other and that for varying periods of three to five years there should be a possibility of sending one or other of these to any of the posts mentioned herein. Professors in training institutions should be enabled for short periods to take up the duties of headmasters or Inspectors so that they may become familiar with the actual conditions of school life and realise how the training that is imparted by them in the training colleges is actually put into practice.

We agree that so far as the nursery and primary stages of instruction are concerned, women are better teachers than men. In regard to Middle schools also a considerable body of opinion is in favour of giving ample opportunities for women to be employed as teachers in these institutions. We agree with this view. In girls' schools obviously women should be the teachers. We have been forcibly impressed by the fact that the education of girls has much leeway to make up. The facilities available for girls in many States are very much limited.

A rapid expansion of girls' education depends to a very large extent upon the availability of women teachers. We have examined this question very carefully and have come to the conclusion that under present conditions it will not be possible to recruit adequate number of women student-teachers in the existing training institutions. We feel therefore that special efforts should be made in this direction. As a short-term policy, at any rate, we would recommend part-time courses being made available to women who could spare a little time and who with the appropriate training take up teaching as part-time workers. Such part-time training may be in the mornings or in the evenings but necessarily the total period of training will have to be-extended. We suggest that three years may be the period for second grade teachers, and two academic years for graduate teachers. The question may be raised as to how they could have practical training on a part-time basis. We think that for the limited time for which this practical training is needed it should not be

difficult to arrange it in such a manner that they can spend their time in the schools concerned. These part-time student-teachers should also be eligible for some stipend during their period of training and if such stipend is given they should undertake to perform the duties of a teacher for a minimum period of three years.

We shall refer to the employment of women as teachers in another part of our Report. We are of opinion that women may be employed as part-time teachers after training and much help may thus be obtained from them if a little more care is devoted to the manner of their employment as part-time teachers.

We would like to stress, in conclusion the importance of the training colleges assuming the role of leadership, in the task of educational reconstruction. Our impression is that they have not so far been able to do so.

They should become active centres not only of research but of practical experiments directed to the improvement of educational methods, curricula, discipline and organization of schools. They should, in the first instance, successfully work out new ideas in their own Demonstration Schools and then, through the example of the school as well as the training given to their students, this influence should permeate into all institutions of the State. At present their work is greatly vitiated by the fact that there is considerable divorce between their theory and practice and the educational ideas advocated in the lecture room are not actually translated in practice in the schools under them. In order to overcome this difficulty, it would be an advantage if each training college could be given the responsibility of supervising the work of a certain number of schools in the neighbourhood, which would, on the one hand, improve their standards and, on the other, enable the members of the staff to give practical shape to their ideas. We are convinced that, if the training colleges could be organized on right lines and become dynamic centres of progressive educational movements, the whole task of educational reconstruction would be greatly facilitated.

3

National Council for Teacher Education

The National Council for Teacher Education (NCTE) was established in May, 1973 by a Government resolution to advise Central and State Governments on all matters pertaining to teacher education, with its Secretariat located in the NCERT. The NCTE's status and role till 1993 have been purely advisory and it did not have statutory powers to enforce its guidelines. As per the provisions laid down in the NPE 1986 and the Programme of Action for its implementation, the NCTE has been conferred statutory status as per the NCTE Act No. 73 of 1993 passed by the Parliament and assented to by the President. It has come into existence with effect from 17th May, 95. The Act provides for establishment of the NCTE with a view to achieving planned and coordinated development of teacher education system throughout the country, regulation and proper maintenance of norms and standards in the teacher education system and for matters connected therewith.

Programmes and activities taken up by the NCTE so for include:

— Preparation of a framework for competency-based curriculum for elementary teacher training institutions.

— Restructuring of pre-service teacher education curriculum for all stages.

— Human Rights and National Values-preparation of materials and orientation of teacher educators.

— Preparation of a video film on teacher training in physical education.

The Status of the Teaching Staff 33

— Preparation of a project proposal on Teacher Education in States/UTs-current status, issues and future projections.

— Development of material for teacher educators on specific subjects.

INSTRUCTORS IN NFE

In the NFE system, the instructor is the key person. The instructor is a nominally paid volunteer who is usually employed on a part-time basis. He/she could be an educated housewife, a girl from the village, an educated unemployed youth, a retired teacher, a qualified social worker, an anganwadi worker or even a professional semi-skilled person. Among the qualities expected of an instructor are dedication to work, and volunteerism. Girls' NFE centres have only lady instructors. The minimum qualification of the instructor is class 10 pass. But studies show that the qualifications of instructors vary from class 8 to Master's degree with a professional degree in education. In fact, there are many remote areas-rural and tribals-where individuals who have studied beyond class 8 are not available. In such cases, the VEC is empowered to relax the minimum qualification of the instructor. In the case of lady instructors, this problem is even more acute.

The basic skill which an NFE instructor is expected to have or develop is multi-class teaching as the group of learners he/she has to deal with is a heterogeneous one. The methodology of teaching at the NFE centre has to be different from the one used in formal schools. Therefore, to orient the instructor in the teaching methodology and also to acquaint him with the content of the learning materials, a four-tier system of training has been developed. A group of master-trainers from each state is trained by the NCERT, who in turn train Project Officers of NFE at the state level. The Project Officers thus trained, are responsible for training supervisors and instructors at the block level.

During the first year, the minimum training period for the instructor is 30 days and in the subsequent year it is 20 days. The first phase is usually divided into three phases and focussed on training in pedagogy, content, evaluation and monitoring. The second phase of training is devoted to discussion focussed at finding solutions to the problems faced by the instructors while teaching at the centre.

Various packages of training materials have been developed to cope with the needs of training. The training of instructors at the district level is done through DIETs. The overall responsibility of training NFE functionaries at the state level rests with the SCERTs.

In the NFE centres, the instructor is the link between the centre and the community and is expected to perform a more dynamic role. He is also expected to take care of the individual needs of the learner and help him/her in solving day-to-day problems. The responsibilities of instructors include the organisation of the daily activities of the centre, identification of out-of-school and non-school going children, the selection of the site for the centre in consultation with the VEC, organising teaching-learning activities by drawing on supervisors, primary school teachers, TLC volunteers, ECCE Centres, the community, nearby voluntary agencies, mobile village library, Block Development Office, Primary Health Centres, etc.

The monitoring of the NFE programme is done on a continuous basis at all levels viz. village, district and state through the VEC, DIETs, SCERTs and Directorate of Education.

The teachers working under TLCs are volunteers and are not paid any salary for their services. Since the qualification of these volunteers is not fixed, any educated person capable of working as a volunteer is appointed and trained. The responsibility of training volunteers of TLCs is that of the State Resource Centres (SRCs).

Conditions of Work

Salary

Good conditions of work play a significant role in attracting and retaining the right type of persons in the teaching profession and enabling them to function efficiently. The working conditions include teacher's salary and benefits, availability of a suitable school building and essential facilities in the school, teacher's workload, method of recruitment, availability of teaching and non-teaching materials and opportunities for promotion.

Today, teacher's pay is probably the most important element affecting the quality of education. The salaries of different levels of teachers are establised separately by each state and are determined on the basis of academic qualifications, training and experience.

In addition to salary, price-index linked 'dearness allowance' is given to all teachers. Various other allowances are also granted to all categories of teachers to compensate them for the special stress under which they work. These allowances are: city compensatory allowance, house rent allowance, hill allowance and other special allowances such as winter allowance, backward, remote and tribal area allowance, island allowance, etc. These allowances differ from state to state and within the state from stage to stage of education. Entry level salaries for trained primary teachers are only slightly higher than those for untrained teachers (e.g., Rs. 90 higher in Karnataka, Rs. 250 higher in Gujarat). The maximum salary for a trained teacher is 3 to 4 times his/ her entry salary, and is achieved only after 1620 years of service in most states.

In the majority of states, the salary scales of trained and untrained graduate teachers in upper primary/ middle schools are at par with those in secondary and higher/senior secondary schools. Teachers with a Master's degree working in higher/senior secondary schools have separate salary scales and are designated as post-graduate teachers (PGTs) or 'Lecturers' (School Cadre).

There is a provision of selection grades for all categories of teachers. Twenty per cent of senior teachers of different categories get selection grades after, 10 to 15 years of service.

In addition, most states provide fixed medical allowance or reimbursement of medical expenses, advances for house building and purchase of conveyance, and free education for the children of teachers, as well as retirement benefits of pension, gratuity and group insurance. In the majority of states, there is also a provision of incentives for some special categories of teachers. For instance, in Assam, Bihar, Gujarat, Maharashtra and Tamil Nadu, a certain percentage of elementary (primary and upper primary) women teachers working in rural and remote areas are given residential accommodation. In some states, physically handicapped teachers are offered conveyance allowance.

Working Environment and Facilities

Working conditions for primary school teachers are different from secondary and higher secondary school teachers, particularly, for those in primary schools in rural areas. According to the fifth all India educational survey 56.25 per cent primary schools, 69.36 per cent upper primary, 72.97 per cent secondary and 89.39 per cent higher secondary schools are housed in buildings. There is a tremendous demand in provision of more facilities such as classrooms and instructional materials. Library facilities are available in only one-fourth primary schools as against 90 per cent in secondary and higher secondary schools.

A plan provision of Rs.500 million has been made in the budget for the year 1996-97 for financing a new Teacher's Housing Scheme under the Central Plan which will be implemented through the State Governments.

It has been observed that teachers serving in remote and inaccessible areas do not have suitable residential accommodation. As a result, they have to commute to their schools from a distance and this affects their punctuality and attendence, adversely. The provision made in this year's budget could be utilised for construction of residential accommodation for teachers in such areas.

Teaching Material

Recent studies at primary level in selected educationally backward districts have revealed. that charts, maps and globes were available in the blocks covered by the Operation Blackboard (OB) Scheme introduced by the

Central Government to provide some minimum infrastructure to primary schools e.g., two classrooms, a kit consisting of some teaching-learning materials and provision of an additional teacher. Teachers in remote areas now handle 2-3 classes, whereas, earlier they used to handle 4-5 classes.

Thus, it is evident that the minimum essential facilities needed for a smooth school functioning and a teaching-learning process need to be upscaled at all school levels, particularly, at primary level.

Other Conditions of Work

Some of the problem areas identified in the teaching field are teacher absenteeism, non-availability of adequate housing facility, frequent transfers, etc.

Workload

The workload of teachers is often judged in terms of amount and type of work done by them. A sample study done by Goyal and Chopra, U. C. Goyal/ and R. K. Chopra, Elementary School Teachers: A Profile, indicates that 42 per cent primary school teachers teach two classes or more at a time. About 50 per cent upper primary/ middle school teachers report that they teach four or more subjects. More than 60 per cent of teachers teach about 50 students on an average, 34 per cent teach between 51-100 and about 5 per cent more than 100 students. This means that on an average about 39 per cent teachers teach more than 50 students in the primary school. At high/higher secondary levels, however, the teacher-pupil ratio was 1:16 in 1994-95. It is evident that there is too much stress on primary school teachers, specially those handling multi-grades.

Education codes in different states specify the number of class or periods teachers at different levels have to teach. A sample study under taken by Goyal and Chopra (1990) further reveals that about one-fourth primary school teachers teach 31-35 class periods and a similar number teach more than 36 class periods a week. In middle schools, nearly half of the teachers teach 31-40 class periods a week, whereas, 12 per cent teach more than 40 class periods.

Besides teaching, elementary and secondary school teachers have to spend a fair amount of time on co-curricular activities, specially in private schools. In addition, teachers have to do clerical work and other miscellaneous work like organising relief work, collecting census data, participating in family planning campaigns, and population control drives, helping in the smooth conduct of elections, etc.

Promotional Prospects for Teachers

In most states, the promotion of teachers in government primary and secondary schools is either on the basis of seniority or seniority-cum-merit. Acquiring higher qualifications also helps in promotion provided a departmental vacancy exists which suits the qualification of the candidate.

In the case of teachers working in private and aided schools, the chances of promotion are rare because in privately managed schools there is a shortage of senior positions and so only one or two persons have the opportunity to reach the level of headmaster/head teacher. In secondary and higher secondary schools, a Trained Graduate Teacher (TGT) may become a Post-Graduate Teacher'(PGT) provided he gets some higher qualifications i.e. a Master's degree in any school subject and depending upon the availability of a vacancy in the school. It may well be that teachers in private aided schools or privately managed recognised schools or public schools remain in the some post from the beginning to the end of their service of 30 to 35 years.

Teachers in government schools can aspire for higher administrative posts in the Education Department of the Government of India. Though a certain percentage of posts in the higher categories of education are reserved for teachers, yet, avenues of promotion in the teaching profession are comparatively more limited than in other sectors such as industry, commerce and business.

Teacher Support Material

A number of agencies such as the NCERT, NIEPA, SCERTs and Departments of Education in universities have developed documentation services for teachers. A number of educational journals addressed to school teachers are published by national and state institutions such as NCERT, SCERTs, Boards of School Education, Teachers' Associations, NGOs and private publishers to disseminate research findings and information regarding innovations attempted by teachers, teachers' educators or researchers in different settings.

Materials (multi-media packages, self-learning materials, etc.) for training and upgrading the knowledge and skills of teachers/functionaries of minority institutions through Distance Education are prepared by the NCERT, IGNOU, NIEPA and NOS, etc.

Some leading newspapers also sometimes bring out supplements or special editions on education. In addition, several institutions and NGOs bring out educational material in audio and video format. Professional associations have also made their contribution in this field. The UGC supports these efforts at the higher education level through a chain of EMRCs (Educational Media Research Centres) and AVRCs (Audio Visual Resource Centres). These efforts are coordinated through a Consortium of Educational Communications (CEC). The IGNOU also has a media programme service. These programmes are telecast throughout the country under the programme 'Country-wide Classroom'. Even though the programmes are targetted at students, teachers are also able to upgrade content and methodology-related delivery and evaluation techniques. Computer software has also been developed to upgrade the knowledge content in various school subjects.

At the school level, the CIET in the NCERT and the SIETs which have been set up in six states are responsible for producing these programmes. Besides these, broadcasts and telecasts cater to regular and out-of-school children and teachers at the primary and secondary level. Several other technological aids and other audio-visual aids have been developed to help teachers in their instructional tasks. A large number of films have also been produced on teacher training, including the teaching of difficult concepts and content areas to children. The films produced include films on the methodology of teaching science, and the needs of children with special problems. Science kits, too, have been developed to enable children to perform experiments related to the prescribed syllabi.

Influenced by the advent of new technologies of communication, the teacher's role has been changing rapidly and teacher education curricula have been revised periodically reflecting this. Interpersonal skills for making instruction interactive and the two-way communication effective have become an integral part of the changes. These curricular reforms have provided teachers an opportunity to participate in the designing of instructional material using locally available resources.

A number of newspapers and magazines extend support to teachers in their work. Many teachers, through their writings in newspapers and magazines, provide additional material to students. School broadcast and school telecast programmes addressed to students of different levels are organised with the help and cooperation of practicing teachers. Teachers participate in the planning, organisation and evaluation of these programmes. Since, these programmes are meant to provide syllabus-based enrichment material to children, they supplement the work of teachers. The government provides a satellite channel to educational and development programmes, the telecast of which is available to students in all parts of the country, This would also give a boost to the development of educational software.

Motivational Efforts for Teacher Development

Private educational establishments-government-aided and government recognised but unaided-make special efforts to maintain their teachers' motivation. Both incentives and disincentives are used. Good work in these institutions is rewarded by giving additional responsibility which is often linked with monetary incentives. In government schools, this is not possible as the head of the institution is not empowered to extend monetary incentives to teachers. Teachers in private education establishments have relatively less security of service. It is relatively easier to dispense with their services if their performance is not found satisfactory. In government schools, though teachers are accountable, teachers' unions make it difficult to enforce accountability, and it is extremely difficult to dispense with their services.

Teachers are involved in the formulation of education policies, development of curricula, syllabi and instructional material. They are also represented on decision-making bodies of universities, boards of school education, SCERTs and DIETs. This is in keeping with the

UNESCO-ILO Recommendation Concerning the Status of Teachers that:

> Teachers' organisations should be recognised as a force which can contribute greatly to educational advancement and which, therefore, should be associated with the determination of educational policy

Moreover, teachers are autonomous in the management of their own classes. They are encouraged to undertake experimentation and action research and are provided incentives both at the state and national level. Every year, the NCERT conducts an All India Competition of Innovations and Experiments undertaken by school teachers and Teacher Educators. Teachers are invited to submit papers on the basis of the work done by them in their schools and as many as 50 primary school teachers and 20 secondary teachers are given national level awards. Similar-awards are also available for elementary and secondary teacher educators.

In the management of educational institutions, teachers at some places enjoy partnership in decision-making. The School Education Acts in vogue in some states have a provision for the membership of teacher representatives on the managing committee of the institution. For example, in the Delhi School Education Act and Rules, 1973, teacher representatives have to be on the managing committee of every recognised school. In the last few years there has been a move that even government schools should have an advisory or managing committee with representatives of the teachers working in the school as members.

To ensure parental support, many schools have either Parent Teacher Associations or Mother Teacher Associations. Parents are invited periodically to the school to discuss the performance of their children with the teachers. In some schools, particularly private schools, parents support the teachers in the organisation of co-curricular activities, art education activities and work experience activities by providing the materials required for these activities. In the DPEP, large scale efforts are underway to facilitate a constructive involvement of parents and the community with the school through the formation of grassroot structures such as VECs, Mother Teacher Associations and Parent Teacher Associations.

Another aspect of enhancing motivation is through the instititution of an annual Teachers' Day, on September 5 "This day is observed in all the schools throughout the country, according a special place to the teacher. Under the aegis of the Ministry of Human Resource Development, a National Foundation for Teachers' Welfare has been set up. This Foundation provides facilities for teachers' welfare.

Table 1 State-wise Enrolment of Students in Higher Education, 1994-95

S. No.	*States*	*Enrolment*	*Increase over the preceding year*	*% increase*	*Average annual compound rate of growth*
1.	Andhra Pradesh	427,652	22,349	5.5	6.1
2.	Arunachal Pradesh	3,240	180	5.9	6.8
3.	Assam	148,170	6,167	4.3	4.2
4.	Bihar	475,230	22,902	5.1	4.7
5.	Goa	16,977	950	5.9	7.3
6.	Gujarat	416,458	18,209	4.6	5.0
7.	Haryana	142,320	6,015	4.4	4.3
8.	Himachal Pradesh	35,354	1,982	5.9	7.2
9.	Jammu & Kashmir	44,752	1,985	4.6	5.0
10.	Karnataka	487,562	25,745	5.6	6.1
11.	Kerala	180,053	7,329	4.2	3.1
12.	Madhya Pradesh	375,216	17,104	4.8	4.8
13.	Maharashtra	950,946	42,051	4.7	5.2

14.	Manipur	28,254	1,359	5.1	5.7
15.	Meghalaya	19,455	1,023	5.6	5.8
16.	Orissa	205,105	10,568	5.4	5.5
17.	Punjab	186,797	10,018	5.7	4.9
18.	Rajasthan	205,215	11,666	6.0	6.1
19.	Tamil Nadu	416,654	23,902	6.1	7.2
20.	Uttar Pradesh	847,263	42,018	5.3	4.2
21.	West Bengal Tripura/Sikkim	354,808	14,331	4.2	3.8
22.	Delhi	136,538	6,453	5.0	5.0
23	Pondicherry	9,910	585	6.3	5.7
	Total	6,113,929	296,680	5.1	5.5

Similarly, with the objective of raising the prestige of teachers and giving public recognition to teachers, the Scheme of National Award for Teachers was launched in the year 1958-59. Primary, middle and higher secondary school teachers are eligible under the scheme. Each award carries a certificate-of merit, cash payment of Rs. 10,000 and a silver medal. In 1993, the number of awards given was raised from 296 to 302.

Higher Education

The enrolment in universities (Table 1) has been on the rise over the post years, with approximately a teaching staff of 0.301 million, catering to a student population of 6.1 1 million students. The pay scales of university teachers have been revised periodically and are considered to be on par with the highest pay scales of civil servants. Benefits include provident fund, residential accommodation (depending on seniority), retirement benefits, etc.

Various incentives exists for teachers to improve their qualifications during their service by way of training and research. They are sent abroad under bilateral programmes of research, area studies, conferences, etc. There are fellowships and scholarships offered by various countries besides travel grants to go abroad. Approximately, 250 scholars visit various countries under these programmes.

Involvement of teachers in decision making is also a vital component of teachers' service conditions. University and college teachers, are involved in the formulation of curricula and the management of university/college affairs. They are autonomous in planning their research. In Autonomous Colleges, teachers have been given the freedom to formulate and teach their courses of general curricula and evaluate their students.

A scheme of Academic Staff Colleges provides training programmes in various subjects as a support for professional development of University and College teachers.

Teachers in Technical Education

With a large network of technical institutions established and developed since independence, and the programmes and initiatives launched in India during the successive plan periods, the technical education system has made significant contributions in producing one of the largest reservoirs of technically trained manpower which has been a source of strength for scientific and industrial development.

The role of teachers in technical education is quite central and crucial. To be effective in their task, the technical teachers have to maintain fine balance between their professional competence and teaching potential. The job of technical teachers is multifarious, 'to guide and inspire the students, to enrich self-discipline, to foster the area of specialisation by keeping abreast of the latest technologies and changing trends and ultimately, to provide services and expertise to the industry and community for finding solutions to real life problems'

The system of technical education has been affected by some crucial issues pertaining to technical teachers which include:

— How to get sufficient number of motivated, dedicated and competent teachers to help produce the required calibre of technical manpower?

— How to create, nurture and retain the inspired cadre of teachers?

— How to select the best talent for the teaching profession?

— How to fill up the present shortage of faculty, and how to face a likely wide gap to be created because of mass scale retirement of senior teachers?

— How to provide challenges, thrills and R&D culture for a holistic development of the technical teachers?

— How to attract brilliant engineering talent, especially, by motivating them during their student age towards the teaching profession as one of the challenging careers?

Schemes and programmes in operation for overall development of technical teachers

The Government of India, over years has taken a series of steps for developing the overall performance of the technical teachers. Significant among them are mentioned below:

Quality Improvement Programme (QIP)

The programme was launched in 1970 with an objective of upgrading the expertise and capabilities of the teachers of engineering colleges and polytechnics in the country, The aspect of upgradation of academic qualifications is achieved with the help of seven major centres located in the IITs, University of Roorkee, IISc., Bangalore and 18 other centre through which the engineering college teacher can acquire their masters and doctoral degree with full salary and allowance. They are also paid a monthly stipend. Over the years, about 2,000 engineering college teachers have acquired Ph.Ds and about 1,700 teachers have acquired masters degrees in engineering/ technology.

The ISTE, a national professional body in technical education conducts summer/winter schools for improving the knowledge, skills and capabilities of engineering college teachers as well as polytechnic teachers. The ISTE conducts a large number of short term courses and programmes at various institutions and industries in the country. The teachers are provided travelling and other allowances as per the rules. So for over 25,000 college level teachers have participated in such programmes and over 4,500 polytechnic teachers have been benefitted under such programmes.

In addition, QIP centres in the IITs, IISc., Bangalore and University of Roorkee also have established curriculum development centres for upgrading curricula of engineering colleges with the help of teachers and experts.

The statutory AICTE has also launched some innovative schemes for teachers of technical institutions which include:

— Travel Grants Scheme

— Seminar/Conference grant

— Career award for young teachers

— Emeritus fellowship
— Professor of Eminence.

Under the scheme of continuing education programmes, presently handled by AICTE, the working professionals in the industry are provided knowledge-based skills and training with the help of teachers of various technical institutions, both at the degree and diploma level. Continuing education has been a very significant aspect of the World Bank assisted project for polytechnics as also the CIDA funded Canada India Institutional Cooperation Project for 12 polytechnics in Southern India.

Despite several measures taken so far, the overall position of filling up the sanctioned posts and attracting competent engineers/ technologists to the teaching profession has been a matter of concern and debate. Efforts are, therefore, afoot to launch some new schemes and programmes for attracting brilliant young teachers by taking them up at a young age and sponsoring them for acquiring higher qualifications. At the same time, designing some new scientific methods of selection and providing adequate research facilities and challenges so as to keep the teachers motivated, professionally satisfied and result-oriented. Several new measures are also required in order to fill up the existing vacancies and the vacancies likely to be created because of mass scale retirement in the near future, especially, in the old reputed technical institutions. The aspects of providing need-based training and also to engage eminent experts as visiting faculty and contract faculty are also being encouraged.

UNESCO-ILO recommendations on the status of teachers in the Indian context

The recommendations concerning the Status of Teachers adopted on 5th October, 1966 by the Special Intergovernmental Conference on the Status of Teachers convened by UNESCO, Paris in cooperation with ILO in 1966 recognised that the document was a unique instrument which recognised that education is fundamental to development and that teachers are the key to educational process. In the Indian context, the major aspects of the recommendations viz. the guiding principles recognises the importance of education and the fact that the status of teachers should be given its due regard in society. This is already incorporated in the NPE.

As far as the educational objectives and policies are concerned the items concerning the interface between the world of learning and the world of work in the field of education is well recognised and has been implemented in India. In fact, the EFA commitment speaks of a financial commitment to the extent of 6 per cent of the GDP by the turn of the century for the education sector.

In the recommendations concerning Preparation for programmes, Educational objectives and policies and Preparation for the profession, there is evidence that there is widespread availability of teacher training facilities as well as comprehensive selection and recruitment facilities for each in the country. The various incentives that are given to employment and career opportunities to teachers have also been well documented. The security of tenure is particularly well established in government run schools.

In the domain of the Rights and Responsibilities of teachers, the Indian context enjoins a fair degree of freedom and flexibility based on a framework outlined by the respective state governments on the issue of freedom of association. In every state, teaching and non-teaching personnel have their unions/associations. These organisations have powers of collective bargaining to secure better service conditions for their members. State level organisations have joined together to form federations of educational organisations for primary, secondary and college stage of education. These federations negotiate with the central government to secure better pay scales and other service conditions. The central question under Indian laws is whether a 'teacher' can be equated to a 'workman', the latter being defined in the Industrial Disputes Act 1947. Various suggestions in this respect are being considered by the Ministry of Labour to amend the Industrial Disputes Act and initiate reforms to grant teachers the same protection as other workers. On the question of the rights of teachers, (in particular, salaries), these are structured as per government norms as laid down by the government from time to time.

On the Conditions for Effective Teaching and Learning, due consideration has been given in the context of the Indian teachers incorporating the recommendations of ILO.

According to NPE 1986, development of Teachers' Code of Professional Ethics has been the responsibility of National level Teachers' organisations and they have themselves evoled such a code.

On the issue of Teacher Shortage and Social Security, there are provisions for various benefits and salary revisions commensurate with inflationary trends that protect the pay of teachers.

It is also a fact that with the expansion of enrolment brought about by active interaction of the government, the requirement of teachers is constantly assessed, monitored and shortages are filled up through regular recruitment procedures.

In short, it may be seen that the spirit and letter of the ILO recommendations have been incorporated in the Indian context and that the status of teachers in India is under constant review to keep pace with the growing and expanding reach of educational opportunities.

TRAINING AND RECRUITMENT OF TEACHERS

The professional skills of teachers in all categories of institutions except the unrecognised ones are determined by the regulations of the state education departments and examining bodies. The level of professional skill required is fixed in terms of academic and professional qualifications which are taken into consideration for granting recognition and affiliation. Therefore, institutions of various types set up in the public and private sectors adhere to the norms prescribed by the state.

Initial training of teachers (pre-service teacher training) is organised at the following three levels, i.e., pre-school teacher education, elementary teacher education, and secondary teacher education

Pre-school Teacher Education

Pre-school teacher education is organised to prepare teachers for teaching pre-school classes, i.e., nursery and kindergarten. The minimum qualification for admission into the pre-school teacher education programme is secondary or senior secondary examination, i.e., 10 years or 12 years schooling. The duration of the course is one to two years. Preschool teacher training institutions are mostly unaided private institutions.

In the case of nursery teacher education and primary teacher education courses, State Education Departments prescribe a minimum percentage of marks in the qualifying examination as a requirement for admission. Some universities have also fixed a minimum percentage of marks in the B.A./B.Sc. examinations for admission to the Bachelor of Education (B.Ed.) course.

Elementary Teacher Education

Elementary teacher education is organised to train-teachers mainly to teach primary classes from I to 5. The minimum qualification for admission into the elementary teacher education programme is either 10 or 12 years of schooling. Recently, most states have prescribed 12 years schooling as the minimum requirement though some states still have the entry qualification as secondary school examination pass. The programme duration in the majority of states is two years, while in others it is one year. Elementary teacher training institutions are of three types-government, private aided and private unaided. Recently, DIETs have been set up in all the states. An important feature of these is that besides ; providing pre-service teacher education, they also provide in-service education to teachers. Thus, both pre-service and in-service education are provided under one roof. The number of such institutes is 424. These institutes are government institutions and are fully financed by the Central Government. The total number of elementary teacher training institutions is 1,179.

Secondary Teacher Education

Secondary teacher education institutes prepare teachers to teach classes 6 to 12. The minimum education required for admission to a secondary teacher education programme is graduation in science, social sciences, humanities, commerce, agriculture, etc. A large number of postgraduates also seek admission to these training institutions.

Secondary teacher education is offered by secondary colleges of education which are affiliated to different universities. Some university departments also offer a secondary teacher education programme. The minimum qualification for admission to this programme is graduation. These institutes are of three types: government, private aided and private unaided. At present, there are around 586 secondary colleges of education.

Four Regional Institutes of Education (RIEs), constituent units of the NCERT offer a 4-year integrated course in secondary teacher education. The minimum qualification for admission into this programme is senior secondary, i.e., 12 years of schooling. Recently, the University of Delhi has also started a four year programme in elementary education leading to the degree 'Bachelor of Elementary Education'.

Teacher education institutions follow the reservation policy of the Government of India with regard to the disadvantaged sections of society like SCs and STs and Other Backward Classes (OBCs). At present, 15 per cent posts in the Education Departments and seats in teacher education institutions are reserved for candidates belonging to the SCs. Likewise, 7.5 per cent posts are reserved for candidates belonging to STs. Recently, 27 per cent posts in all services including teaching have been reserved for candidates belonging to OBCs.

Curriculum for Teacher Education

The primary teacher, specially, in the first three grades is expected to teach mainly literacy, numeracy and life skills. Besides these, the teacher is required to have knowledge of the process of a child's growth, development and learning. At the secondary stage, a teacher is expected to be familiar with adolescent psychology and social processes, in addition to knowledge of school subjects.

The curriculum for primary teacher education is developed by state governments/State Boards of Teacher Education and is reviewed from time to time. The curriculum for secondary teacher education developed by universities is also reviewed and updated periodically in the light of changes in the school curriculum, advances in pedagogical science, societal demands, technological advancements and changes in the socioeconomic structures in the country.

The NCERT has developed model curricula for elementary and secondary teacher education. State governments and universities may adopt/ adapt this in their teacher education programmes. The NCERT revises these curricula from time to time. The latest curriculum brought out in 1991 for both levels has the following components:

— Foundation Courses

— Education in Emerging India

— Educational Psychology

— Stage Relevant Specialisation

— Elementary Education and Teacher Functions

— Language Teaching

  — Teaching of Mother Tongue

  — Teaching of English Language

  — Teaching of Mathematics

  — Teaching of Environmental Studies (Science)

  — Teaching of Environmental Studies (Social Studies)

  — Teaching of Health and Physical Education

  — Teaching of Art

  — Teaching of Work Experience

— Additional Specialisation

  — Science Teaching/Social Studies Teaching/ Pre-school Education.

    — Elective-one :

- — Adult Education
- — Non Formal Education
- — Social Education
- — Tribal Education
- — Multiple Class Teaching
- — Population Education
- — Special Education
- — Educational Technology'
- — Practicum
- — Practical Work

— Internship in Teaching (in Primary and Upper Primary/Pre-school Systems).

The weightage for different components is mentioned below:

Foundation Course	20%
Stage Relevant Specialisation	30%
Additional Specialisation	10%
Practicum	40%

It is evident from the weightages mentioned above that the pedagogical component has received a weightage of 80 per cent in the curriculum. The curriculum lays a great deal of emphasis on teaching through child-centred, activity-based and cooperative learning approaches. Enriching the trainee's knowledge of the content of school subjects is also an important objective of the curriculum.

The components of the secondary teacher education curriculum are the some as that of the elementary teacher education. There are, however, variations in courses depending on the stage for which the teachers are prepared.

Teacher Training for Special Needs

To look after children with special needs, the NPE 1986, recommended integrating children with locomotor and mild disabilities in general schools. The implementation of the UNICEF assisted 'Project Integrated Education of the Disabled' (PIED) in ten demonstration sites in different contexts further encouraged policy makers to integrate children with moderate disabilities in general schools, The Multi Site Action Research Project also promoted the need to develop 'effective' schools for all. All these experiences focus on the preparation of the general school system to meet the special needs of not only those with physical impairment but also of those with mental impairments and learning disabilities.

A provision has thus been made by the NCERT to orient all teachers and education officers by incorporating a component on special needs in all major inservice training programmes. The emphasis is on preparing general teachers and also moving towards the organisation of primary schools as inclusive schools focussing on meeting individual needs in the classroom. Teachers receiving this training are supported by multi-category trained teachers who were, provided training by 4 RIEs of the NCERT. Teachers absorbed into special schools, mostly single disability schools or those with multiple disabilities such as spastics, cerebral palsy, etc., are trained under the guidance of the National Institutes for the Handicapped as well as some non-governmental organisations with courses accredited by the Rehabilitation Council of India. A number of universities have also started offering B.Ed., and M.Ed., courses in special education.

Recruitment of Teachers

Different states follow different recruitment procedures.

In some states, the recruitment is made on the basis of the candidates performance in a competitive examination, whereas, in some other states, recruitment is made on the basis of the academic and professional background of the candidate. The merit of each candidate is determined on the basis of his/her score in the examinations he/she has passed in addition to previous teaching experience, if any. In some other states, a combination of the two procedures, i.e., performance in a competitive examination and merit determined on the basis of academic credentials is adopted, Some weightage is given to the performance of candidates in an oral examination held through interviewing the candidates.

The qualifications required for the recruitment of Lecturer in a university/college are:

- Qualifying in the National Test conducted by the UGC or any agency approved by it.
- A Master's degree with of least 55 per cent marks or its equivalent grade and a good academic record.

At the higher education level, 45 Academic Staff Colleges are involved in teacher training and university departments also organise orientation programmes and refresher courses.

Institutional Infrastructure for Training

The infrastructure for in-service training of teachers exists at the central, state, regional, district and sub-district levels. At the national level, there are the NCERT, the NIEPA, the Central Institute of English and Foreign Languages (CIEFL), Hyderabad, and the Central Institute of Indian Languages (CIIL), Mysore.

At the regional level, there are Regional Institutes of Eduçation located in the four regions of the country- Northern, Western, Eastern and Southern. One Regional

Institute has been set up recently at Shillong for the states in the northeastern part of India.

At the state level, there are the SCERTs, State Institute of Education (SIE), State Institute of Science Education, IASE, CTEs, SIETs.

Districts have DIETs and In-service Training Institutes. DIETs cater to the in-service education of teachers working at primary and upper primary level. In-service education of secondary teachers is being looked after by CTEs. It is proposed to strengthen 200 CTEs, of which 73 have already been established. The IASEs are looking after the in-service education of senior secondary school teachers, including principals of these schools and the faculty of DIETs.

Recently, in-service training centres have been set up at sub-district level, i.e., block and cluster level. To begin with, these centres are being established in the districts covered under the DPEP.

National Policy on Education and in-service training of teachers

In the context of the NPE 1986, the Government of India formulated a national scheme of in-service training of teachers to reach out to primary and secondary school teachers. The objectives of the scheme known as the Programme of Mass Orientation of School Teachers (PMOST) was to sensitise teachers to the emerging concerns in education, UEE, use of learner-centred approach, action research, the emerging role and responsibilities of teachers, enrichment of their knowledge in curricular areas, and other thrust areas enlisted in the NPE. The duration of training was 10 days. The programme was in operation from 1986-90 and about 1.8 million teachers were covered by it. The training programme was strengthened by media support. Films relating to various modules constituting the training print package were telecast on the national network for the benefit of teachers in different parts of the country. Each viewing session was preceded and followed by discussion. A participatory, interactive approach was followed in the training. The programme was implemented by the NCERT in collaboration with the SCERTs in different states.

After the PMOST, another programme/scheme known as the Special Orientation Programme for Primary School Teachers (SOPT) was launched from the year 1993-94 to improve the quality of primary/elementary education as part of the strategy to achieve UEE. The main focus of this programme is implementing the MLLs identified for the primary stage, training in the use of Operation Blackboard materials provided to primary-school teachers, and encouraging teachers to adopt a child-centred approach to teaching. It envisages covering 0.45 million teachers every year. During the past few years, these two schemes of moss orientation have covered more than 2 million teachers. Like PMOST, this programme too, is strengthened by media support. Films on various themes covering the course design are shown to teachers during training programmes.

In most of the states, pre-service teacher education is essential for appointment as a teacher. Therefore, most states do not organise induction programmes for new entrants. However, some organisations like Kendriya Vidyalaya Sangathan and Navodaya Vidyalaya Samiti do organise a short induction, programme for newly appointed teachers.

Training for Addressing the Needs of Disadvantaged and Minorities

In-service programmes are organised to realise three objectives-awareness, content upgradation and fine-tuning of teaching skills. The duration of a course differs from the others depending upon their nature, objectives and content.

At present, the in-service education of teachers through distance mode is organised on a very limited scale. In-service education is mostly provided through face to face modality. However, recently a programme has been developed to provide in-service education to primary school teachers through distance education mode in the districts covered under the DPEP in which a multi-media approach would be used. The programme will be implemented by the IGNOU in collaboration with the NCERT. Recently, NCERT has successfully experimented with using interactive teleconferencing for training of Primary teachers of Karnataka and Madhya Pradesh, This intervention will be upscaled as an important strategy for in-service education.

Besides sensitisation to general problems and priorities of education, the in-service training of teachers is also focussed on specific areas requiring different kinds of competencies. These specific competencies include educating groups with special needs like SC and ST children, disabled children and those belonging to minority communities. Since, these groups have different social, linguistic and physical problems, training and orientation programmes for key persons and teachers working with them have been formulated keeping these in view.

From time to time, the NCERT provides orientation at the national level to key persons working for the education of SCs. This orientation is used by them during the training and also during the orientation programmes they organise for teachers of their states associated with the education of the SCs.

The Welfare Department/Tribal Development Departments in the states, and the UGC through the state colleges also organise remedial programmes to enrich and facilitate teachers working in the areas predominantly inhabited by the SCs and STs.

Training programmes addressed to teachers working in educational institutions of minority groups are in the formulation stage and will be implemented in the coming years. However, as a start, NCERT has designed some orientation and training programmes to help educationally backward minorities. Steps have also been initiated to update the list of minority concentration districts and these shall be made available to voluntary agencies and SCERTs requesting them to include teachers/functionaries of minority schools from these areas in their training programmes.

From the standpoint of promoting integration based on the appreciation of the national goals and ideas in conformity with the objectives of the core curriculum, a study on the analysis of curriculum in terms of specified MILLs at the primary stage is being undertaken.

Innovations: Large and Small, Rich and Varied

The lost decade has seen a number of innovative efforts in all spheres of school education. Underlying these is a desire to evolve feasible as well as desirable models that may eventually grow into larger scale solutions. Many of these efforts have significant bearing on teacher education practices, especially those that can lend themselves to larger scale implementation. As will be seen from a select list of more recent efforts Wow, innovative efforts are under way in governmental as well as non-governmental organisations, and in different parts of the country.

Ekalavya, Madhya Pradesh

Easily among the most important of innovative projects, the Primary Education Project of this organisation involved a group of resource persons-curriculum developers, teacher trainers and material developers—teaching for a year in the place of teachers in typical interior rural government primary schools, in order to understand the context in which teachers teach.

The teacher training programme evolved in tandem with curriculum and materials over a period of five years. This is a participative, organic and experiential programme, rooted in the nature of the actual conditions in which teachers have to function. After field testing in 25 schools for a further three years, the programme now covers over 104 schools. The teachers who were trained initially now comprise the majority of the trainers.

Digantar, Jaipur (Rajasthan)

Starting as a rural school just outside Jaipur, this innovative project/programme views the multi-grade and multi-level learning situation as an advantage, and often has children from primary and secondary levels working together. In addition to developing materials, this organisation has worked on non-formal and alternative education, as well as on teacher training. A specific aspect of the work on alternative education is on ensuring the appropriate flexibility to adapt the learning situation to the context of the community for which it is meant, while preserving a strong element of academic rigour. This social orientation and academic rigour also inform the teacher training evolved by Digantar, which is running in various forms in Rajasthan and Madhya Pradesh.

Rishi Valley Education Centre, Chittoor (Andhra Pradesh)

A rural extension of the Rishi Valley school offering

support to nearby schools, this programme soon had to contend with the multigrade situation, in which a large number of teachers found themselves. The Rishi Valley team, therefore, evolved graded self-learning material which allows both the child and the teacher to monitor the progress of learning. However, they then successfully went on to train teachers in hundreds of schools to use this material to cater to their specific situation. At present, Rishi Valley has emerged as a major resource of educational effort, particularly, in multi-grade teaching in all parts of the country.

Lok Jumbish, Rajasthan

This large scale programme truly attempts to involve the community and establish decentralised resource groups and centres for teacher support. A special emphasis is on such structures of the block and cluster level. Training and constant upgradation of skills and knowledge base of the resource groups is an ongoing process. Teachers' attendance in training programmes is entirely voluntary (and is usually more than 85 per cent!).

M V Foundation, Andhra Pradesh

An organisation active in the field of education of child workers, M V Foundation organises regular 'camps', where working children find a supportive, stimulating atmosphere in which they learn a surprisingly great amount in the short duration of three months. Though there are no monetary incentives for parents sending their children to the camps, the demand for these camps has grown dramatically, as also the number of volunteers or motivated teachers. A very high percentage of children who attend these camps acquire a minimum learning level as well as the motivation to go back to school. One of the key reasons for this success is the nature of the relationship established between teachers and children during the camp.

UP Basic Education Programme, Uttar Pradesh

A large scale programme running in 10 districts of Uttar Pradesh, this programme had to encounter the difficulties of training over a short duration. With help from national resource organisations such as the NCERT, the UPBEP evolved a training programme that was 'trainee friendly" used self-learning training material, and focussed initially on language learning, rather than on the whole gamut of the curriculum. By breaking down the training programme into manageable parts, the overall training process too became more practicable, ensuring optimisation of the efforts of both the trainer and the trainee.

DPEP, Assam

A major problem confronting this north-eastern state was the absence of resource institutions and individuals. Hence, a serious effort was made to select trainees from among teachers who could then be trained to become trainers. This selection process was both rigorous (taking into account, for example, acceptability among fellow teachers, positive attitude, aptitude, etc.) and transparent. In addition to specific training programmes, monthly meetings of teachers are used to provide inputs in keeping with the academic difficulties experienced by them. A key factor in this effort has been the creation of a feedback mechanism and a district level Academic Resource Group which responds rapidly to teachers' needs as they emerge.

DPEP, Kerala

Overhauling its training programme from a lecture-dominated experience, the DPEP in Kerala has successfully made a turnaround to more participatory training methods. A significant aspect of this was that the master trainers had no central module or training package with them. Instead, each trainer had a 'My Own Training Manual'-a folder containing key questions on training, with space to be filled in by the master trainer during an orientation workshop, in light of the context in which she/he would be training teachers. Teacher response from the training programmes then conducted indicated that trainees found the training 'practical', so much so that they now wanted a 'different' kind of teachers' handbook. Feedback from teachers played a considerable role in the development of these new teachers' handbooks, Like the training manual, these handbooks too are 'personalisable'-in other words, they are complete only when the teacher fills in spaces left specifically for her/him to contextualise the handbook.

Centre for Learning Resources, Pune, Maharashtra

Set up as a resource centre to support efforts in early and primary education, the Centre has resources for materials development and training of teachers, as well as supervisory staff. Especially rich in mathematics material for primary school, the Centre has recently developed material for the education of tribal children, a particularly difficult area of work.

Bihar Education Project, Bihar

Following a review where training had been identified as a weak area, this project evolved an entirely new and extremely motivating training programme, focussing, especially, on social sensitisation of teachers.

A greater understanding of self and community is generated through experiential exercises and intensive, open discussions. Preliminary assessment has already recorded a significant decrease in absenteeism among teachers. A highly participatory exercise, this training often leads to teachers' ongoing inputs and support towards improvement in their pedagogical skills.

Math Learning Group, New Delhi

Essentially, comprising interested academics from different disciplines who have teamed up with a number of willing teachers, this group has been exploring ways in which mathematics can be made less 'frightening' as well as enjoyable and a rich learning experience. Teachers have, in addition to participating in academic discussions and training, been field testing methods in municipal schools, with documentation being undertaken to record outcomes.

Srujanika, Orissa

This NGO has focussed on science learning, especially among rural children and has involved hundreds of teachers in various activities such as science fairs, bal melas (children's fairs), and events around phenomena, such as the recent solar eclipse. The effort is to generate both a scientific temper as well as for learning joyfully in such an exploratory fashion.

Shikshak Samakhya, Madhya Pradesh

A Teacher Empowerment Project sponsored by UNICEF, Shikshak Samakhya encompasses teacher training, generating resources for the school, especially, through community participation, and administrative support. Teachers start with a one-day training, focussed on building motivation and providing guidance in the preparation of learning materials, followed by monthly sessions at the school cluster level. Each teacher receives

Rs.500 from UNICFF as well as Rs.2,000 from the community (panchayat) funds towards improvement of school facilities. Local educational and administrative officials are also involved, so that red tape is reduced and attention is drawn towards teachers' problems. Thus, the programme works towards improving the school environment and teachers' morale, self esteem and the will to improve teaching.

Shiksha Karmi, Rajasthan

Shiksha Karmi Project (SKP) aims at universalisation and qualitative improvement of primary education in remote and socio-economically backward villages in Rajasthan, with primary focus on girls. Identifying teacher absenteeism as a major obstacle in achieving the objective of UEE, the project substitutes local voluntary workers for regular primary school teachers. This project has achieved remarkable success in improving enrolment (300 per cent), attendance (58 per cent to 85 per cent) in the participation of girls and most importantly in mobilising community participation.

4

Education for Personality Development

The 1972 Report of the International Commission on Development of Education, had become very famous during the seventies, but it has unfortunately receded into the background. To know, to possess and to be – this is the central demand of life, and, rightly, this ought to be the central demand of education, particularly when, as in the Report, there is a clear and categorical recognition of the need for a fundamental identification of life and education. As the Report states in the very first principle of 21- point programme for a global strategy in education:

> "Every individual must be in a position to keep learning throughout his life. The idea of lifelong education is the keynote of the learning society."

But, as we begin to seek for the meaning of life-long education and its central theme "to be", we are confronted with a number of implications which in their turn centre round the idea of personality and personality development. As M. Edgar Faure, the Chairman of the Commission, states, one of the underlying assumptions of the Report is "that the aim of development is the complete fulfilment of man, in all the richness of his personality, the compexity of his forms of expression and his various commitments."

But there are controversies regarding what constitutes personality and the real meaning of the full richness of personality. There are also controversies regarding the conflicts of the demands of personality development with those of professional efficiency. There are also pressures of society to demand men of professions rather than men of developed personalities. Contrarily, there are assertions in favour of personality development against the pragmatic necessities of their professional excellence. And then there is a deeper issue as to whether the fullness of personality can be achieved in the present state of society and civilisation. Indeed, education for personality development seems to necessitate not only a revolutionary change in the aim, content and structure of educational institutions, but also a revolution in the entire object, mode and interrelations of social existence.

For us, what is most significant is the logic of the new educational methodology which reinforces at every turn the need to place the child and its personality at the centre of entire edifice of education. The modern educationist has come to realise that the child is not a plastic material to be moulded and pressed into a shape as desired and decided upon by the parents and educators. There is an insistence on free choice for the student to choose his own subjects of study, his pace of progress, and even (within limits) his teachers. There is a recognition of individual differences, necessitating variation in psychological treatment, presentation of materials of study, and criteria for judgement of performance. There is a demand for new syllabi and for flexible syllabi which would correspond to the psychological needs of the growth of the personality abolition of the examination system, and need, therefore, to discover a more rational and psychological system that can replace the system of tests, checks and counterchecks. All these demands and needs point to the idea of education for the all-round development of personality.

But what is personality? And how to prepare ourselves for the education for personality development? Personality is sometimes identified with character, but very often a distinction is made between the two. According to this distinction, character means the fixed structure of certain recognisable qualities while personality means the flux of self-expressive or sensitive and responsive being. But when we examine the distinction between the fixed structure and the flux, we find that the fixity and the flux are only relative terms, and in the movement of Nature, nothing is fixed. Personality may then be regarded as a plastic expression of certain forces and ends of Nature combined for the time being. Deeper psychological research affirms, as in the system of Yoga, that this combination of forces can be disturbed, it can be modified, it can be totally changed. Personalities can be multiplied within the same individual; the conflicting personalities in the individual can be harmonised; one can become capable of putting forth the needed personality according to the circumstances or the demands of the work or situation, even while the other personalities would remain behind, contributing to the efficacy of the personality put in the front. One can even go beyond all personality and know the real person that assumes so many personalities.

One can make a distinction between the real Person and the instruments of the person, viz. the body, life and mind. And between the person and the instruments there is what one might call the force of the person that expresses itself and gives a special turn, a special power of configuration, a certain stamp to the instruments. It is this special stamp or power of configuration that gives rise to the specific formation of a pattern of qualities and drives to our body, life and mind. It is that which we should call properly 'personality'. In the language of the Samkhya psychology, we might say that body, life and mind are the expressions of Prakriti marked by the three gunas: *sattva, rajas and tamas.*

The normal human being is simply an instrument of *Prakriti,* dominated largely by *tamas* or *rajas,* expressing indeed some pattern of these qualities, but as yet unable to become aware of the inner person, *Purusha.* In the Samkhya, the *Purusha* is a mere Witness which is inactive, and it is not proper to speak of the Force of the *Purusha.* But in the Vedanta, especially in the original Vedanta of the Upanishads, and in some of its best developed forms, the inner person has its own force, often called the soul-force, which when awakened, pours itself into the instruments of *Prakriti,* and it is this meeting of the Soul-Force and *Prakriti* of Nature that causes the real formation of Personality.

The greater the opening of Nature to receive the flow of the Soul-Force, the greater is the resultant personality, and the fullness of Personality would be achieved initially by full development of mind, life and body under the sovereign guidance, rule and will of the Soul-Force, and a complete coursing of the energies of the Soul-Force, into the stuff, vibrations, activities, modes of mind, life and body, into the movements of *sattva, rajas* and *tamas,* with the power of their complete refinement, change and transformation.

The Soul-Force vibrates with the power and presence of the inner person, the true individual, which is quite different from the ego, a product of Nature or *Prakriti.* The true individual is called, in Sanskrit, the *Chaitya Purusha,* the one which is described in the Upanishads as *'no bigger than the thumb'.* It is, indeed, no bigger than the thumb when there is as yet no awakening in us of its presence and its force, but it is that which grows in us in answer to the needs of our internal and external growth, and the secret of all development of personality lies in that presence and in its force. It has, therefore, been affirmed that if one wants to develop the needed personality or wants to have mastery over one's own personal development, and even of the circumstances of our development, then the right method is to discover and seek a living contract with that inner person. In the absence of this contract, one will always remain subject to the formations of qualities in oneself, and will have no power to control, guide and perfect these formations. It is, therefore, concluded that the fullness of personality can come about only by the complete emergence of the inner person and the full expression of its force.

This force has, if we study closely, four basic expressions. It expresses itself through four Powers: a Power for knowledge, a Power for strength, a Power for mutuality and active and productive relation and interchange, a Power for works and labour and service. Accordingly, we have four basic personalities: the personality of knowledge, the personality of strength, the personality of harmony and the personality of skill.

"The psychological fact is", says Sri Aurobindo, "that there are these four active powers and tendencies of the Spirit and its executive Shakti within us and the predominance of one or the other in the more well-formed part of our personality gives us our main tendencies, dominant qualities and capacities, effective turn in action and life. But they are more or less present in all men, here manifest, there latent, here developed, there subdued and depressed or subordinate, and in the perfect man will be raised up to a fullness and harmony which in the spiritual freedom will burst out into the free play of the infinite quality of the spirit in the inner and the outer life and in the self-enjoying creative play of the Purusha with his and the world's Nature-Power."

The full richness of personality is the splendid, opulent and marvellous integration of the four-fold personality. The full heart of Love is tranquilised by knowledge into a calm ecstasy and vibrates with strength; the strong hands of Power labour for the world in a radiant fullness of joy and light; the luminous brain of Knowledge accepts and transforms the heart's obscure inspirations and lends itself to the workings of the high-seated Will. All these powers are founded together on a soul of sacrifice that lives in unity with all the world and accepts all things to transmute them. This, we may say, is the condition of man's integrality.

Such then is the basic idea of the integral personality and the process of its formation. In this idea we find the completion of several other ideas of personality of the. remedy of dangers presented in several processes of exaggerated formations of egoism and individuality. According to one conception, personality is identified with egoistic individuality having a certain sense of ends or values. And fullness of personality in this sense would mean an enlarged development of egoistic individuality by means of an increased power of mind, an increased power of vital force, by a refined or dense and massive exaggerations of the forces of what Yoga calls 'Ignorance'.

This would manifest even a violent and turbulent, exaggerated, vital ego, satisfying itself with a supreme tyrannous or anarchic strength of self-fulfilment. Or, it would manifest a mighty exhibition of an overpowering force, self-possessed, self-held, even an ascetically self-restrained mind-capacity and life-power, strong, calm or cold or formidable in collected vehemence, subtle, dominating, a sublimation at once of the mental and vital ego. These are indeed superhuman manifestations, but even on a lower key, these manifestations are appalling, and one shudders at the idea of personality development if such is to be the result of education for personality development.

There is, of course, an idea of a harmonious development of personality in which body, life and mind are developed integrally and with a kind of balance that would avoid exaggerations of the vital or mental ego. Something of this kind was attempted as an ideal in the early Greek culture, and this is often proposed all over the world as a salutary aim for education. At its highest, it attempts a harmony of the triangular disposition of the individual, a harmony of the aesthetic, ethical and rational tendencies. The highest ideal that is formulated is that of the pursuit of the Truth, Goodness and Beauty.

But modern psychological studies have revealed the tendencies of intrinsic conflict of these three ideals as understood and practised by the human mind. There have also been revealed the tendencies of the unconscious which constantly bombard the shifting harmonies of personality, and the researches made in the fields of parapsychology reveal deeper complexes and compactions whose harmony is extremely difficult to achieve. What we call harmony is most often a compromise of tendencies, an apparently working order concealing under a brittle cover a mass of uncontrolled and unregenerate or unregulated impulses, tendencies, dreams, imaginations, systems of ideas and motives. There is, in fact, a sort of controlled disequilibrium, but not a happy mastery of a rich harmony.

The inner soul, the inner person of the Indian psychology, has an inherent power of purification and harmonisation. It detects the error and falsehood spontaneously; it turns effortlessly to all that is noble and mysterious and wonderful. The development of personality that is accompanied with or initiated by an awakening to this inmost soul, this psychic entity, prevents egoism and exaggerated formation of egoism; it harmonises effectively the aesthetic, the ethical and the rational. It has even a power to transmute the passions and impulses; it can even set right the subconscious and open it to the supreme light by which it can finally be transformed.

> "It is", in the words of Sri Aurobindo, "this secret psychic entity which is the original Conscience in us deeper than the constructed and conventional conscience of the moralist, for it is this which points always towards Truth and Right and Beauty, towards Love and Harmony and all that is a divine possibility in us, and persists till these things become the major need of our nature. It is the psychic personality in us that flowers as the saint, the sage, the seer; when it reaches its full strength, it turns the being towards the Knowledge of Self and the Divne, towards the supreme Truth, the supreme Good, the supreme Beauty, Love and Bliss, the divine heights and largenesses, and opens us to the touch of spiritual sympathy, universality, oneness."

The coming forward of the psychic person marks a momentous stage in the development of personality. It then begins to govern overtly and entirely our outer nature of mind, life and body, and then this can be cast into soul-image of what is true, right and beautiful, and in the end, the whole nature can be turned towards the real aim of life, the supreme victory. A transformation of the mind, life and body by the presence and the power of the psychic being is effected. This process may be rapid or tardy accordingly to the resistance in our developed nature.

But ultimately, by the greater and greater infusion of the psychic light, every part of the being is psychicised. As Sri Aurobindo describes it :

> "Every region of the being, every nook and corner of it, every movement, formation, direction, inclination of thought, will, emotion, sensation, action, reaction, motive, disposition, propensity, desire, habit of the conscious or subconscious physical, even the most concealed, camouflaged, mute recondite, is lighted up with the

> unerring psychic light, their confusions dissipated, their tangles disentangled, their obscurities, deceptions, self-deceptions precisely indicated and removed; all is purified set right, the whole nature harmonised, modulated in the psychic key, put in spiritual order."

There are, still, according to Sri Aurobindo, higher levels of consciousness, ranges of the powers of the fourfold personality in the superconscious. These ranges are those of what Sri Aurobindo has termed the Higher Mind, the Illumined Mind, Intuitive Mind, Overmind and Supermind. An account of all this would form a subject by itself, and in an introductory paper as this we cannot dare enter into this field.

What we need to stress now is that the secret of personality development is an awakening to the psychic person and the development of body, life and mind in such a manner that they might aid in this awakening and might become well-trained instruments of the fourfold personality of knowledge, strength, harmony and skill.

It should be evident that the personality development as conceived here is a life-long education. And yet, it is a process that must begin right from the earliest stage, and must determine the drift, the content, and method of all our stages of education. And it seems inevitable that an education motivated by the development of personality demands a radical change in our approach, attitudes, methods, structure, system of evaluation, of syllabus and of contact with the students.

And, first, we may ask if we could find some principles which would guide us in our work of organising some practical organisation of education for personality development. In a series of articles that Sri Aurobindo wrote in 1909-10, as a leader of Indian nationalism, in order to expound what he conceived to be the lines on which a system of National Education could be evolved, he enunciated three fundamental principles to which reference is made earlier.

There are several other guidelines that we find in Sri Aurobindo. While explaining the instruments of the work of the teacher, he writes in his Synthesis of Yoga,

> "Teaching, example, influence, - these are the three instruments of the Guru. But the wise Teacher will not seek to impose himself or his opinions on the passive acceptance of the receptive mind; he will throw in only what is productive and sure as a seed which will grow under the divine fostering within. He will seek to awaken much more than to instruct; he will aim at the growth of the faculties and the experiences by a natural process and free expansion. He will give a method as an aid, as a utilisable device, not as an imperative formula or a fixed routine. And he will be on his guard against any turning of the means into a limitation, against the mechanising of process."

"What is his method and his system?" asks Sri Aurobindo and answers,

> "He has no method and every method. His system is a natural organisation of the highest processes and movements of which the nature is capable. Applying themselves even to the pettiest details and to the actions the most insignificant in their appearance with as much care and thoroughness as to the greatest, they in the end lift all into the Light and transform all."

"This imperfect nature of ours", explains Sri Aurobindo, "contains the materials of our perfection, but inchoate, distorted, misplaced, thrown together in disorder to a poor imperfect order. All this material has to be patiently perfected, purified, reorganised, new-moulded and transformed, not hacked and hewn and slain or mutilated, not obliterated by simple coercion and denial."

These principles, it will be observed, are subtle and complex, and no rigid formula of practice can be derived from them. They impose a great responsibility on the teacher and demand from him extraordinary qualities of a profound psychologist.

It would also seem that the education governed by these principles stands in need of a very flexible structure or organisation, in which the paramount place is automatically assigned to the varied needs of student's growth. In such a system, it is not merely the 'subjects' of study that should count. A much greater importance will have to be assigned to the inner aspiration, experience of freedom, possibility of educating oneself, self-experimentation, discovery of the inner needs and their relation with the programme of studies, and the discovery of the aim of life and the art of life.

A great stress will fall upon each student's individual work, and there has to be subtlety in forming flexible groupings of the students.

Our present structure of education is imprisoned within the walls of a triple system, and if we wish to make education for personality development a practical proposition, we must examine this triple system in some depth and suggest some practicable solutions. This imprisoning system is the lecture system, syllabus system, and the examination system.

We may begin with a few remarks regarding the Lecture System. A lecture or a speech as a creative expression of the inner spirit is a living vibration and it has an indispensable place in any ideal system of education.

Again, a lecture which is an informal talk has also an important place in education.

Also, lectures have a great utility in (a) introducing a subject, (b) stimulating an interest for a subject, (c) presenting a panoramic view of a subject, (d) explaining general difficulties or hurdles which are commonly met by a large number of students in their studies, (e) creating a collective atmosphere with regard to certain pervasive ideas, and (f) initiating rapid and massive programmes of training.

Finally, lectures as reports of research work have their undeniable place and value. But where the above aims or conditions are absent, lectures become dry, boring, ineffective, irrelevant to the interests of the students, and therefore useless.

Also, instead of being given a legitimate and rightful place, lectures in the present system are given almost a central place. It has been regarded as the central task of teachers to lecture and to cover the syllabus through their lectures. As a result, teachers are most often uncreative in their lectures; they are in a hurry to pour out their knowledge without much regard for the interest and attention of the students. Students tend to remain mostly passive, often inattentive and become in due course restless, and even violent. The present lecture system is thus quite unpsychological and devoid of much educational value. This must be changed radically.

Next, we may examine the syllabus system with which our lecture system is so closely connected.

A syllabus as an over-all view of an idea of a subject has necessary place in any ideal system of education.

A curriculum as an instrument of certain goals to be achieved has also an important place.

Also, a syllabus has a great utility in presenting to the student the various elements involved in what he is going to learn, in stimulating his interest in those elements, and in creating in him a 'prospective' attitude towards his studies.

Also, a syllabus as an instrument of a graded system of learning has its value and usefulness (at least in some areas of studies).

But a syllabus cut out rigidly and fixed uniformly for all the students alike is a heavy chain that smothers the innate tendencies of curiosity, variation, digression, play and spontaneity. It also cuts across a genuine development towards the synthesis and globality of a wide sweep of integral comprehension.

A wrong notion also grows that only what is given in the syllabus is that which is to be learnt; what falls outside the syllabus is often ignored and remains ignored indefinitely.

Instead of giving a legitimate place to the syllabus, it has come to be regarded as a backbone of the entire structure of the educational system.This situation must radically change.

A syllabus as a general panoramic view in the vision of the teacher and as a guideline for the student has a legitimate function, and this function has to be preserved. But in the actual operation of the educational process, there have to be what may be called 'evolutionary' syllabi. A syllabus should grow according to the needs of the inner growth of the student, and the student should be free to develop and weave the various elements of his studies into a complex harmonious whole on the lines of his deeper quest and according to the rhythm of the inner flowering of his personality.

We should aid at progress, but at free progress. We should aid at perfection, but a perfection that is a spontaneous and happy flowering.

The progress of the student has to be related to the motivation of the student. Curiosity as a motive has to be fostered and nourished. It has to be deepened and enlarged. But a time must come when mere curiosity is transformed into a serious search after the Truth. It is this transformation that marks a real progress.

A time comes in the process of learning when the student is awakened to the necessity of mastery or perfection. When this motivation begins to operate, more and more thorough programmes of training can be proposed, for it is with this motivation that training becomes a rigorous but joyous exercise.

Many of the difficulties of the teachers in dealing with the students arise because most programmes of study are programmes of training, and these are presented to the students whether they are psychologically ready or not.

There has to be a long period of general culture during which attention is to be paid to the cultivation of deep interest and love for studies and a large and wide grasp of the world and its mysteries. Stress on specialisation and mastery and perfection has also to be there, but a serious attention to this aspect should be given, it seems, only when the motivation for it begins to arise in the consciousness of the student.

All this implies a new handling of the students and their interests. It also implies the paramount importance of the observation of students and a deep psychological understanding of their motivation and their needs of growth.

A sound principle of teaching is, as we have noted elsewhere, that the child should be consulted in his own growth, and so, instead of imposing a programme of studies, the teacher has to work with the student pointing out to him the various paths of progress and asking him to choose what he would like to pursue. The teacher can certainly guide, counsel, help in choosing, but he should not impose.

It is true that finding a vocation and the necessary training for the chosen vocation are indeed important motivation of study, and they have to be given an important part in our total scheme. But we have at first to note that the chief vocation of man is to be Man and to transcend the limitations of manhood. And the key to the making of a Man is to develop the faculties of original, subtle, and complex thinking capable of seizing the heart of things and men and events, and the will-power to control and harmonise the various impulses, instincts and desires by means of the perception of a noble ideal and an unfailing resolution to realise that ideal. There has also to be a full growth of the body and its powers of strength, agility, plasticity, health and grace. And all this development of the body, life and mind is to be under the guidance of a secret knowledge and was the privilege of India to have once possessed in a great measure, and she can now recover and develop it even in a greater measure. This is the knowledge of the psychic and the spiritual.

Whatever else may be the vocation of the individual, to possess this knowledge of the inner spiritual being and to guide his mind, life and body in the light of this knowledge – this has to be chief programme of the vocation of every student. A wide, special and flexible syllabus for the discovery of and training for this vocation has to be the major concern of New Education.

But this chief programme has also to be related to each student for the specific role that he has to play in the world- activities.

A psychological handling of the student reveals the fact that every child has in him the materials for his perfection but these materials are in an undeveloped state or they are ill- organised. The specific role and vocation of each is intrinsically related to the harmonisation and perfection of these materials and to the natural and right rhythm of this process of perfection.

It will also be found that each man's natural vocation is intrinsically related to a natural tendency towards the mastery of a specific Technology, if we use that term in its widest sense in which not only scientific technologies but also language and law are included in its connotation. It is this natural tendency towards technology that should be encouraged right from the early stages of education. And for this purpose, there should always be available ample facilities for the cultivation of interests in various technologies and for their mastery in due course.

But care has to be taken to see that the study of technology does not become mechanical. And to prevent this we must realise that technology is a tool of expression. This would mean that the over-all emphasis should fall upon the inner springs of self-development which would necessitate expression, and which ; in turn, would necessitate the use of tools of expression.

It is also to be noted that while technology is oriented towards utility, and therefore all technological training has to be for serving certain utilities of life, the ultimate aim of technological training should not be 'utilitarian' in its vulgar sense. The aim of technology is and must be to be the vehicle of the expression of an ideal, an aspiration, an inspiration and a perfection.

A new organisation and syllabus for Technology would result from the above considerations.

And now we come to the Examination System. Tests as means of judging achievement are necessary and often indispensable. As such, they have an important place in any ideal system of education.

Tests are also useful for stimulation, for providing opportunities to the students to think clearly and formulate ideas adequately, for achieving precision, exactness, for arriving at a global view of the subjects of study, for self-evaluation, and for gaining self-confidence.

Tests can also be a matter of fun and play. But tests as a threat and as a means of securing the students' motivation for studies are a barbaric misuse of a useful instrument.

Tests coming as they do only once in a year in a decisive way, the uniformity of tests in disregard of the individual differentiation, an almost exclusive reliance on written tests which encourage cramming or unreflective reproduction of the material read or studied – these are among the elements that hurt the sensitivity of psychologists and educationists whose hearts yearn to foster the minds and hearts of the students with deep understanding, tenderness and affection in relation to the psychological needs of their growth of personality.

The fact that even a silly, mechanical mind can pass the tests, and that too with honours, is sufficient to pass a verdict against the present system of tests.

The fact that the most important aspects of culture that we wish our children to cultivate lie entirely beyond the scope of our tests is sufficient to show what a marginal place tests should occupy in our total system of education. The great values of truthfulness; sincerity, cheerfulness, benevolence, right judgement, sacrifice, friendship – these are some of the things which we wish our children to possess. As these do not come under the sweep of the examination system, they tend to be neglected or ignored or given a very inferior place in the educational process. But it is these rather than many other superficial things that should have a sovereign place. Means must be found by which sovereign things achieve their sovereignty.

The examination system must be radically changed. The motivation for studies has to come from a natural curiosity, a sense of inner need of a profound quest, and an inevitable necessity for the search after the Truth and Perfection. The teacher's genius will be judged by the way in which he can give the right and timely contact to his students and provide the necessary nourishment to their curiosity and need for a quest or stimulate them by striking ideas, projects, stories, and daily conversations, and much more by example and influence.

Let not tests be a substitute for these profound and deep things which constitute the very heart of education. There are what may be called 'romantic' periods of study and they come to different students at different stages of development, These are the periods of general expansion or a passion for a given preoccupation or falling in love with education. These are the periods entirely unsuitable for tests.

There are others when students need to clarify their vague ideas and sentiments ; they need precision and system. These are the periods when oral or written tests appropriate to these needs can be given.

There are again periods of assimilation at the end of which there is need to review in a connected manner the different elements of study. Here tests for comprehension or an extensive exposition would be relevant.

There are also periods when there is a will to undergo a rigorous programme of training. During such periods, even a series of difficult and strenuous tests would be perfectly justified.

Tests would be particularly needed where the courses of Technology (understood in its largest sense) are concerned.

Tests have thus to be a varied nature, and for each students, tests must come to such a way that they are helpful to his growth.

Tests must not be the means of passing or failing, of promotion or detention, but means of a self-evaluation, stimulation, and for correction and perfection. Moreover, tests may be oral or written or practical, according to the need and circumstance. It is also to be realised that impromptu tests can be more effective both in their power of stimulation and in arriving at a right judgement of the actual capacity of performance of the student.

It will be seen that in this view of tests, there will be no need to prefix any time-table for tests; they should be given to the students as and when necessary.

In any case, it has to be realised that the right way of judging a student and his progress is by an inner contact, an inner feeling for the student, an inner tact and discrimination. These qualities have to be developed by the teachers. And it is when these qualities are developed that they will vibrate in the atmosphere a power that encourages and nourishes the great virtues of the inner soul of the student.

These considerations suggest some lines on which a new organisation for New Education suitable for personality development could be evolved. But before we come to further precisions, it may seem necessary to state some over-all propositions regarding the spirit in which the new organisation should function, and the general role of the teachers in this New Education.

There will be, it may be said, four features of New Education :

> A sincere pursuit of the Truth, persistent seeking of an organisation of progressive Harmony, and a spontaneous Freedom fulfilling itself through growing order and perfection.

Informality in instruction, joy in learning, utter dedication, strictness in training, and the widest comprehension in the student-teacher relationship – these will govern the new methods of education.

An ever-fresh youthfulness, a constant prospective thrust towards New Future, and a happy thirst for continuous progress – these will govern the atmosphere on New Education.

A search for the highest aim of life, a stress on the integral development of personality, and a living expression of the unity of mankind – these will be the universal preoccupations of the teachers and students.

In New Education, students will not go to schools and colleges in order to listen to lectures, but for a quest, for finding out the answers to their questions, for consulting the teachers, when needed.

The very disposition of the classes will be radically changed, so that students have facilities to consult the teachers for a short or long time according to the needs. Instead of their being at the head of the class, the teachers will be found at convenient places so that they are readily available to those who need them for help, guidance, consultation.

The teacher's main occupation will be to observe his students, their inclinations and capacities, so as to be able to help them with deep sympathy and understanding. One of his important activities will be to write out something special for each of his students which will be useful for his general and specific growth. This involves a great deal of research work, but that is the privilege of his station in life.

The teacher will not be a mere lecturer; rather he will be an animator. He will inspire much more than instruct; he will guide by example and by the influence of his inner soul and its noble aspirations.

To aid the student in awakening the inner will to grow and to progress – that will be the constant endeavour of the teacher.

To evolve a programme of education for each student in accordance with the felt needs of the student's growth, to watch the students with deep sympathy, understanding and patience, ready to intervene and guide when necessary, to stimulate the students with striking words, ideas, questions, stories, projects and programmes – this will be the main work of the teachers.

But to radiate an inner calm and a cheerful dynamism so as to create an atmosphere conducive to the development of the higher faculties of inner knowledge and intuition – that will be regarded as the very heart of the work of the teacher.

As hinted earlier, there are, it seems, two important stages or aspects in the process of learning, the aspect of what may be called 'culture' and that of what may be called 'training'. The two are indeed interlocked, and in such a complex process as that of education, it is impossible to make clear-cut distinctions and compartments. An yet, it seems important to make some pragmatic distinctions, and some definite provisions for these two aspects.

Both these words 'culture' and 'training' have certain associations, and they need to be clarified after a detailed discussion. For our present purpose, however, we shall attribute to the word 'culture' that process of learning which is a result of a spontaneous and natural growth of faculties, capacities and personality by virtue of an easy stimulation of the environment, or a happy and attractive influence, something that may in a way be described as a leisurely growth of genius. And by 'training', we shall mean the process of learning which involves regular, persistent, methodical, rigorous and meticulous exercises. This occurs where the natural growth has reached a high point of maturity which demands a further development of precision, clarity, efficiency, and over-all perfection. It is also needed sometimes or often where the inherent urge is either absent or not so prominent, or else where there is an obstacle or a blockade in the growth. Or, again, there may be a need to stimulate an interest or capacity which is not active, either because it is only latent or it is absent. Or, finally, it may be needed where there is a mere laxity due to inertia and indifference.

If we examine them carefully, we shall find that most of our educational methods aim at providing some adequate-inadequate aids which are pertinent only to the aspect of training. But since they do not apply to the stage or aspect of culture, there is an artificiality in the atmosphere, and there is an undercurrent of a psychological revolt on the part of the students.

In the New Education, this defect must be eliminated. For this elimination, it seems, two things are needed.

Firstly, there must be on the part of the teacher a recognition that:

— Education must be a happy process, and happiness is a fruit of the inherent urge to grow, unhampered by external pressures.

— All educational processes must aim at achieving this happiness among the students. And all help, guidance and facilities should be provided towards this end.

— The right method of education has therefore to be that of 'culture', and all processes of training should gradually or rapidly be transformed into those of culture.

However, where this transformation has still not taken place, the right time for the programme of 'training' is when the student feels inwardly the need for clarity, precision or perfection, and when he is willing to impose upon himself an outer discipline for a short or long period) (according to the needs of the situation) of vigorous and persistent (or even repetitive) exercises.

In the absence of this inner will, there may be a need to impose outer discipline; but this imposition should be only a temporary device, and the aim should be to eliminate it gradually and totally. In any case, the imposition from outside must not be arbitrary and should not be offensive to the sensitiveness and sensibility of the students.

Secondly, for purposes of organisation, it may be convenient to have different organisations for 'culture' and for 'training', with a kind of flexibility so that students can use these organisations easily according to the psychological needs of their growth.

All programmes of 'training' should be conducted in what may be called 'Laboratories'. Normally, we have laboratories only for natural and applied sciences; and the normal work there is called 'practicals'. Recently, with the advent of language laboratories, the conception has gained in connotation, and we can, for our present purposes, enlarge it still further. Thus, we might propose that there should be laboratories for each branch of knowledge, and these laboratories might be organised in about the following way : Information will be available here about:

— what the subject in question means, and why it should be studied;
— a few alternative syllabi for the subject;
— an analysis of the various steps involved in the learning of the subject systematically and thoroughly;
— an idea of the different ways of preparing for these various steps.

There will also be available here :

— selected standard and reference books related to the subject;
— interesting and stimulating booklets or story books and other relevant documentation pertaining to the various topics of the subject;

— programmed books pertaining to the subject; these books often need to be supplemented by what may be called 'Work Sheets', i.e. educational material so prepared that it can be studied only by student's intelligent reflection and application. These work sheets should be of various types to permit alternative approaches;

— a series of graded exercises which the students can handle on their own with the least help from the teacher; (there should be a facility for self-correction);

— various kinds of test papers, including what may be called 'final test papers'; (these final test papers are those which the students under training may be required to answer in order to judge for themselves if they have achieved the necessary mastery).

The following activities will be encouraged :

— determination to work hard, work regularly, and to develop the habits of punctuality and discipline;

— to fix up a short or long programme of work, and to stick to it rigorously (laxity in this may disqualify a student from the joining of the given programme of the laboratory work);

— to arrange, from time to time, a short programme of lectures and seminars where a number of difficult problems will be discussed and dealt with rapidly and effectively;

— to give written reports of the work done;

— to pass certain tests (written, oral or practical);

— any other activities to achieve clarity, precision, efficiency, mastery.

We may now suggest a few ideas for the organisation of the stage or aspect of culture or of spontaneous and natural growth. Every student is normally in this stage with regard to most of his activities and returns to it after every short or long period of growth by training. He is often in this stage in regard to most of his activities simultaneously with his being in the other stage with regard to one or more of the other activities.

This is the interlocking of the two stages, and therefore, many of the features envisaged for laboratory work should more or less be available for what we have called 'cultural work'. But in cultural work, there will be a stress on freedom, a sense of leisurebness, a natural rhythm of work, daily conversation, and easy passage from one activity to another, fostering of interests and 'romance' of learning, warmth of friendliness and free collaboration in work, joy of discovery and invention, deep and profound reflection, spontaneous meditation, creative expression, fun and frolic of exercise, free consultation and discussion, development of consciousness, growth of spherical thought and action. These elements should also be present in the 'laboratory work', but there the stress will be on rigour, measure and mastery.

An adequate organisation of the 'cultural work' will need the following rooms :

— A Room or Rooms of Silence to which students who would like to do uninterrupted work or to reflect or meditate in silence can go when they like;

— Rooms of Consultation, where students can meet their teachers and consult with them on various points of their seeking;

— Rooms of Collaboration, where students can work in collaboration with each other on projects, etc.;

— Rooms of Exhibition, where students can organise various exhibitions of their work, — charts, plans, paintings, etc.;

— Hobby Rooms, where students can work freely on various hobbies, such as aeromodelling, carpentry, fret-work, etc.;

— Rooms for Dancing, Music, Paining, Dramatics, etc.;

— Lecture Rooms where teachers can hold discussions with their students and where they can deliver lectures - short or long, according to the need;

— Store Rooms where materials for exhibitions, hobbies, etc., can be stored carefully and systematically.

We may call these Rooms 'Halls of Culture' and it may be suggested that all these Halls as well as Laboratories should be quite contiguous in location so that there is not much movement from one place to another.

And now, a few ideas may be suggested which will describe the actual working of New Education. It is necessary to point out that while the New Education will be proposed for general acceptance, it will not be imposed upon any one. Having ensured this basic assumption, the following points may be suggested for the actual operation of the work :

— There will be no compulsion with regard to any subject of study;

— The choice of a subject for study will be freely made with each student, and this choice should reflect a real and serious quest of the student;

— At the beginning of the session, students will be invited to indicate what lines of study or what particular topics they would like to explore;

— In order to facilitate the choice of topics, teachers may present to the students a suggestive but detailed list of suitable topics; teachers who may so wish, may also give a few talks to the students to explain the main outline of their subjects in order to stimulate their interest; students may also be advised to consult the material available in respect of laboratories to have a detailed idea of the various subjects;

- Each topic thus selected will constitute a short or a long project according to the nature of the topic;
- In exploring each project, students will take the help of the teacher or teachers whom they might choose from among those competent to deal with it;
- Teachers, on their part, will endeavour to relate the exploration of the projects to the inner needs of the students and the methods of exploration will be so organised as to permit the cultivation of intuition and higher faculties of knowledge and action;
- In guiding students, teachers will be expected to endeavour to widen and intensify the area of exploration so as to avoid narrow specialisation or mere idle superficiality;
- Normally, students will work in the Halls of Culture but, according to the needs, students will be permitted or recommended to join laboratories for a given topic or subject;
- Each student's programme of studies will be flexible, supple and evolutionary;
- In the selection of topics of study, students will not be restricted to any single faculty;
- There will be no lecture classes fixed in advance for the whole year. But teachers may arrange, by agreement with their students, lecture classes when necessary particularly in relation to the 'laboratory' work;
- Lectures will be confined to their legitimate and justifiable purposes indicated earlier;

— The over-all duration of various courses operating at present in the ordinary system need not be changed;

— Tests will be given to the students, when necessary, particularly in relation to the 'laboratory work'; tests will be confined to their legitimate and justifiable purposes as indicated earlier;

— At the end of every two or three months, each student will submit to the 'Coordinator' a report of his work in regard to each topic or subject. This report will give details of the progress he made in regard to what he has read or written or the reflections and the conclusions which might have been reached. It will also give an account of various activities in which he may be engaged whether under the supervision of the teachers or not. No activity will be regarded as extra-curricular, since all activities will be a part of education and of his programme of self-development;

— These reports will be transmitted to the Coordinator through the respective teachers (or directly where in regard to certain activities work is done without the supervision of any teacher). In doing so, they will mention the students' regularity of sustained effort, development of capacities, understanding of their subjects and the power of answering questions orally, practically or in writing with sufficient clarity and precision;

— Teachers will also give help by suggesting if a given student needs to do laboratory work in regard to a given topic or subject;

— The quality of the work will be considered more important than the quantity of the work, although the latter should not be meagre, but commensurate with high standards.

It will be seen that in this working, a special emphasis falls upon individual attention and upon providing necessary facilities for the maximum development of each student. There will thus be a great stress on 'individual work'. The individual work may be pursued in several different ways:

— by quiet reflection or meditation;

— by referring to books or relevant portions of books suggested by the teacher;

— by working on 'work-sheets';

— by consultations or interviews with the teachers;

— by carrying out experiments;

— by solving problems;

— by writing compositions;

— by drawing, designing, painting, etc.;

— by any other work, such as decoration, cooking, carpentry, stitching, embroidery, etc.

At the same time, there can be several situations in which a 'group work' is desirable and necessary. There are a number of projects in which there can be a division of labour and the need for the coordination of the work done by the participants; there can be educational games of team work, and there are often needs for joint exploration and experimentation, joint pursuit of a subject, useful lectures. In all these cases, collective work is very useful, and it should be encouraged.

But care should be taken to see that the needs for individual excellence are not sacrificed for the sake of the demands resulting from the consideration of the economy of the collective work. Often the collective work tends to be mechanical, and this tendency should be discouraged. It is preferable that the collective works are of a short duration of one or two months at a time. Longer periods may be needed in relation to 'laboratory' work, but in the determination of the general working of the individual and group work, there should be no rigidity. Grouping is best done when it is encouraged to be formed spontaneously on the basis of natural affinities of character of personality. The organisation should constantly grow so as to make the working supple and plastic.

It will also be seen that in this working there is no compulsion with regard to any subject of study, and the student will be free to choose any combination of subjects and to progress at his own pace. At the same time, this imposes upon the student a good deal of discrimination and an intimate understanding of the process of education itself. The aim of education, the value of different subjects of study, the need for mastery and perfection, and the psychological process by which one can develop one's own personality are some of the most important and difficult things on which students have to reflect deeply in order to take intelligent decisions with regard to their progress.

It should be the function of the teacher to provide to the students all the necessary elements of information and material relevant to these important questions and to present them in their full perspective.

In doing so, the following recommendations may be useful :

— *Learning by practising:* One of the great defects of learning through reading and through books and lectures is the gulf that has been created between theoretical knowledge and realisation by experience. Much of our knowledge is theoretical, and we do not know how much of it is really true in experience; much of our knowledge is abstract, and we do not enjoy it as a matter of deep and intimate possession

> of our very being. Much of our knowledge is ineffective, impotent, and we do not know in experience that knowledge is Power; much of our knowledge is a burden, and under the weight of the 'explosion' in knowledge, we do not know how to master knowledge, how to look 'steadily and whole'.

This situation is due to the fact that we have lost the real art of learning; for the secret of learning is, as was known to the ancient seers, the experience which comes by an inner and sincere practice.

To know what is the Truth, one must practice the Truth in words, thoughts and actions. To be able to posses the Truth, one must practice day and night self-control and self-mastery.

There are, as the ancients declared, states of consciousness in which the necessary knowledge occurs intuitively; and it is the knowledge occurring in the right consciousness that is effective and fruit-bearing. Not that knowledge as information is not important; for all operations of action, precise and detailed information is indispensable; but information received by mere listening or reading is most often a dead burden or a source of our imprisonment within narrow grooves and partial beliefs and opinions.

Information must grow from consciousness, and paramount importance must be given to the growth of profound and sincere states of consciousness rather than to the feeding of information.

And these states of consciousness come by an intense aspiration to know, by a great calm and silence, by stopping of the chattering noise of words and turmoil and riots in the mind. And this means a constant, persistent and steady practice of concentration and purification.

This process can greatly be aided by inner and outer action, by a process of creativity, by a process of experimentation and productivity. If we examine life closely, we find that every circumstance of life has a message in it. Life is the great teacher of life. Every incident of life can be a field of experimentation of inner or outer action. Our attempt should be to cultivate the right attitude towards life-situations and derive from them the educational experience proper to the need of our growth. We are here on the earth not merely to be deep and wide in our consciousness, but also to deal with outer situations, to control and master them, and also to create situations appropriate to the needs of our inner growth and our internal and external perfection.

A good teacher will always utilise daily situations of the student's life and turn them into occasions for the inner art of learning.

In recent times, there is a great awakening to the value of learning by doing. A number of programmes and projects are being suggested to use as stimulation which would evoke active responses. A great stress is being laid on learning through craft and manual work, works of production and experimental exercises, handling of material and technological occupation. There is also a powerful and salutary movement to utilise creative activities such as art, music, dance, composition of poetry, prose, drama. All education is, it is contended, ecstasy that comes from creativity.

All these ideas are undoubtedly excellent, but often each one of them is made into an exclusive gospel of right education, and in stressing this activity or that, the inner heart of learning is missed, namely, the growth of inner consciousness, inner concentration, and inner life of sincerity. Outer action may and often does help the inner; the outer perfection has undoubtedly to be a part of the total; but the foundation has to be inward, and if this is not centrally understood and practiced, there is in the end bound to be a failure.

Search for meaning and unity of knowledge: There is fundamentally no subject which is not interesting, and there is no subject which is not immediately or remotely related to any other subject.

A subject is uninteresting only so long as it is not sufficiently understood, and nothing is understood unless everything is understood.

And yet, when we pursue everything we are led into an endless movement and we seem to be drifting away somewhere towards a greater vagueness and incomprehension.

We are baffled by multiplicity, variety, endlessness. There are details and details, and there is a constant explosion of knowledge. We are in a stage of constant disequilibrium. We seem to have no standing ground.

Is there a secret knowledge knowing which everything can be known? The ancient Upanishads affirm such a Secret Something. But it is neither this subject nor that subject, nor it is all subjects put together. And yet it is in every subject, and in all subjects. In a sense, to learn this subject or that subject is not so important, nor is it important to learn the interrelation of subjects. The important thing is to learn and understand that Secret. That Something is the Meaning of Meaning, the Meaning of this, or that, of all.

The method of learning That is an entirely inner process. It cannot really be taught. One can only awaken to it and realise it. No learning is that awakening, and yet all learning can be made an occasion for that awakening.

Three things may be suggested as an aid to this process of learning:

(a) Whatever be the subject of topic on hand, there should be a constant endeavour at 'understanding', 'comprehension' To get at the heart, at the meaning to grasp, to hold it in the centre of consciousness, — this should be the primary indispensable operation of learning.

(b) Not to limit or narrow down to a limited number of subjects, but to encourage the development of interests for larger and larger fields of knowledge and activity, constant enlargement of interests, faculties and frontiers of knowledge, — this should be a necessary general operation of learning.

It is this enlargement that brings the perception of the inner meaning of all. We begin to perceive that there is in every field and all fields taken together an essentiality, universal generality or commonness, and an endless variety of particulars, details and uniqueness.

All superficiality is a waste of time and energy; to do something and not to do it well betrays an insincerity which is the enemy of all progress. Therefore, while enlarging interests there should be a measure, so that the multiplicity of activities does not necessitate superficiality or inadequate attention. To do a thing as quickly as possible and as perfectly as possible gives us the right measure and balance.

A great help in this process is the growth of panoramic view of the world, a synoptic vision of the whole, the spherical thought, spherical consciousness.

(c) The third aid is the development of skill of perfection, efficiency, speed of performance, mastery. This should be a consequential operation of all learning. There may be here a selection of a limited number of fields and, in certain circumstances, where there is a need to invention and some pioneering work, even narrow specialisation. But even here, the stress will be on the discovery of That, the secret Something. Given this motivation, this stress, the defects of specialisation will intrinsically be corrected.

In recent times, a greater and greater need for specialisation is felt, but also a greater sense and value for enlargement and for general education. To arrive at some satisfactory solution, two things have been suggested.

(1) Man, it is said, is the best subject of study for Man. And in the study of man, it has been argued, we have all the wideness and generality that we need and hope for.

There has thus grown the idea of 'core' or 'common' subjects of which the study of Man or some humanistic study form an indispensable part. This study is proposed as an obligatory study in the syllabi of various humanistic and technological courses.

(2) The second powerful and salutary idea is that of an inter-disciplinary approach to studies. A stress is laid upon the perception of connections, relations, the underlying unity of knowledge.

These are, indeed, excellent ideas, but they are often thought of and presented as a real remedy for our complex and difficult problems of curricula and syllabi. But the psychology of education is subtle and does easily make itself subservient to rigid formulas. Such an attempt is therefore not likely to be the final solution.

A good teacher will no doubt regard man and his future, his circumstances and the events that shape his destiny as extremely important, and will undoubtedly underline the necessity and importance of the study of Man, but he will not impose it.

A good teacher will no doubt encourage the study of multiplicity of subjects and interdisciplinary approach, and he will take care to see that it does turn into an artificiality and superficiality. He will see that globality of thought and sphericity of thought are encouraged; but he will permit them to grow naturally and spontaneously. He will not impose them in the form of a logical web.

He will remember constantly that he is not a teacher of a subject or subjects, but a helper in the search after the Meaning of Meaning of Meaning, the secret of the Unity of all knowledge.

Perpetual Education and Perpetual Youth

A constant aspiration for progress and perfection, a thirst for progress and a zeal, *utsaha,* for self-perfection, should govern the rhythm and law of self-development. To progress constantly is to remain young perpetually, and constant progress comes by perpetual education.

To limit the hours of education during the day and during the year, to organise education on the idea of finishing it one day, to bifurcate education into curricular and extra-curricular courses, to regard studies as work and games, as mere play and pastime, to give exclusive value to reading, writing, reasoning and eloquence, and to regard all else as secondary or as mere decoration - these tendencies are inimical to the conception of all life as education.

We have fear of time and space. We want our children to get at the certificates as soon as possible. We want them to elbow their places in a limited corner of the world fraught with merciless competition. We want them to be 'settled' soon, somewhere in a 'comfortable' place

There are indeed many sociological reasons for these fears and anxieties. But the root cause is that we do not ourselves live for a new future; we wish to 'sit down', to gravitate to some kind of sleep.

In recent times, however, new ideas of life-long education and of integral education have begun to dominate forward-thinking educationists and sociologists. They advocate a freer and larger use of time; they discourage the idea of 'finishing' education. They maintain that there should be no compulsion to finish a course within a specified period, there should be no compulsion to pass the tests, there should be no 'promotions' and 'detentions'.

These are excellent ideas, and they should all find a place in New Education. A good teacher will not prescribe a course, he will allow it to evolve; he will not give tests, he will stimulate an ever-growing progress.

But he will also take care to see that there is an awakening to the ocean of Time and to the secret and calm Eternity that causes constant progression.

To live in eternity and to live for constant progression is, it is said, to be left for mystics and for some extraordinary individuals But the time has come when that mysticism and extraordinariness are demanded even of us.

The significant fact is that the idea of Evolution is spreading everywhere, and in this idea is the force for perpetual education We are gradually becoming aware that evolution itself can evolve, that Man himself is an evolutionary laboratory. To study our own evolution, to aid this evolution is to liberate ourselves from stagnancy. A good teacher will, therefore, purpose a project an Evolution to all his students; all else, all other studies and activities will form part of this major and all embracing study. In this study are contained the implications of perpetual education.

It is in this context that we have to permit our students to progress at their own pace and on the lines of their self-development. But what about jobs? What about occupations? How and when will the students be fit, we shall be asked, for their work, their job? But our experience shows that the students, if they are free to choose their pursuits very much like to be carpenters, masons, decorators, cooks, technicians, linguists, surgeons, managers, pilots, chauffeurs. And with this free pursuit, they will work out their natural inclinations and be fit in good time for the professions of their choice. But how much fear is born of the fact that we want our children not to be carpenters, musicians, dancers - we want them to be doctors, managers, lawyers, engineers! We have ourselves false values and hence the entire system is saddled with false demands, and the result is a vicious circle.

The secret of our profession lies in our personality; but personality is not a fixed entity; it is a vibration of qualities and attributes durable for a certain season of experience; it must change with the growth of experience and with this change of personality the profession, the work and its scope must change also. A poet need not remain a poet all his life, throughout every phase of varied experiences; a surgeon needs very often to paint and philosophise; a philosopher needs often to be a warrior and a statesman. A mystic may need to be a charioteer in a battlefield.

It has been pointed out that the entire domain of the secrets of the growth of personality has remained ignored, and the consequence is that most of us possess smothered personalities, and most often we are engaged in a work that has no correspondence with our real genius, with our inner delight of existence. Most of us live in deep conflict, alienated from ourselves.. It is this inner conflict which causes ageing, and even in our youth we feel so old and worn out.

But as we have noted elsewhere, we shall strive to perceive still deeper, to fathom into secret of the true person, behind all personality, and seek there the real power of solving our conflicts and integrating different personalities. This is a deep and precious wisdom, the self-knowledge which reveals that the secret of perpetual youth is not a mere progression, but a deeper art of progression, namely, the constant harmonisation of our outer work and circumstances with the inner needs of the manifestation of the powers of the real Person seated deep within us.

It is this secret of eternal youth that will be the inner soul of New Education.

This education will insist on the development of the mind, life and body; it will so develop them as to make the instruments of the discovery of the inner psychic being and ultimately as instruments of the perfect manifestation of the inner and higher realities. The effort will be to make the body supple, strong, agile, and beautiful; the vital will be trained to be dynamic, disciplined, obedient and effective; and mind will be cultivated to be intelligent, observant, concentrated, rich and complex. But at every stage, the paramount importance will be given to the needs of the psychic and spiritual growth. As the Mother writes:

> "The will for the great discovery should be always there soaring over you, above what you do and what you are, like a huge bird of light dominating all the movements of your being."

5

Integral Education

In the history of the development of education, we find in certain systems of education a stress on harmonious development of the physical, the vital and the mental aspects of personality. Such, indeed, was the Greek ideal of education, which has reappeared in the modern West, and which influences the modern educational thinking in India. It has also been recognised that there have been systems of education laying great stress on the building up of the character and on the inculcation of moral virtues. In some systems of education, an attempt has been made to provide for the study of some religious text and for some religious practices. There is also a tendency to suggest a system of education in which all the above elements would, in some way, be incorporate.

There are, however, certain important developments which necessitate a clearer and a more radical concept of integral education.

Firstly, there is, today, an unparalleled width and depth of inquiry, which requires a new kind of education that would simultaneously be comprehensive and specialized or varied so as to suit each individual. Secondly, the modern human personality has become, as never before, subject to psychological turmoil, imposing a new dimension in education that still remains undefined and insufficiently explored. Thirdly, there is a greater quest all over the world for the synthesis of knowledge and culture. Ancient knowledge is being rediscovered in the context of modern knowledge. The humanist and the technologist are finding themselves in greater and greater need to each other ; and the scientist and the mystic are getting ready to embrace each other. The educational implications of these developments are obvious. Our educational syllabi have to reflect the latest trends of synthesis, and our educational objectives must include the idea of preparing a new kind of man who can consciously and progressively harmonize within himself the broad vision of the humanist and the skill of the technologist, the disciplined will-force of the moralist and the refined imagination of the artist, scrupulous knowledge of the scientist and the sublime vision, wisdom and ever-growing perfection of the mystic.

At a still deeper level, we have the most profound concern of our times, namely, that of an unprecedented crisis which can be considered evolutionary in character, a crisis that occurs in a species at a time when some kind of mutation is imminent. As Sri Aurobindo declares :

> "At present mankind is undergoing an evolutionary crisis in which is concealed a choice of its destiny ; for a stage has been reached in which the human mind has achieved in certain directions an enormous development while in others it stands arrested and bewildered and can no longer find its way. A structure of the external life has been raised up by man's ever active mind and life-will, a structure of an unmanageable hugeness and complexity, for the service of his mental, vital, physical claims and urges, a complex political, social, administrative, economic, cultural machinery, and organized collective means for his intellectual, sensational, aesthetic and material satisfaction. Man has created a system of civilization which has become too big for his limited mental capacity and understanding and his still more limited spiritual and moral capacity to utilize and manage, a too dangerous servant of his blundering ego and its appetites. For no greater seeing

> mind, no intuitive soul of knowledge has yet come to his surface of consciousness which could make this basic fullness of life a condition for the free growth whole-being, whole-knowledge, whole-power is needed to weld all into a greater unity of whole life."

If human existence were of one piece, solely material-vital, or solely mental, or solely spiritual, problems of human life would not have reached the kind of criticality that we are facing today. But the human being is a triple web, a thing mysteriously physical-vital, mental and spiritual at once, and not knowing what are the true relations of these things, we have been let to a situation where we are obliged to listen to the conflicting voices and their imperatives, and we do not know what to follow and what to reject. Against this background, deeper questions both of life and education have become extremely urgent and imperative.

The first danger in this situation is a resurgence of the old vital and material primitive barbarian in a civilized form. This danger is likely to overcome humanity if there is no high and strenuous mental and moral ideal controlling and uplifting the vital and physical man in us and no spiritual ideal liberating him from himself into his inner being. Even if this relapse is escaped, there is another danger. For there may come about a crystallization into a stable comfortable mechanized social living without ideal or outlook. The present world situation seems to be fast developing into that kind of crystallization over larger and larger areas of the world. Rational thought can, indeed, if it continues to develop on higher and higher domains, prevent this peril. Unfortunately, the rational thought of today is still disinclined to mediate between the life and the body on the one hand, and something higher and greater within the human being, the spiritual reality, on the other. In that situation, humanity may succumb to the comforts of mechanized social living and may even succeed in burying the deep call of the spirit. This burial would mean perilous suffocation of evolutionary urge to arrive at the fullest possible perfection of the individual and the society and the perfection of the relationship between the individual and the society.

Self-exceeding or self-transcendence is the fundamental law of the nature of the human being, and if humankind comes to the paralyzing situation where the urge to exceed the limits of the mental human being is buried under the heavy weight of the civilization of comfort and pleasure, of continuous competition and conflict and of disabling appetites of egoistic life, controlled by dehumanizing machinery of civilization, then the human being will have frustrated the purposes of evolution, and those powers which lie at the summit of the possibilities of human personality. This is the heart of evolutionary crisis, and this crisis can be averted only if we are able to work at the highest frontiers of human resources and open up the gates of the forces and powers which lie beyond these frontiers in the realm of the Spirit.

One favourable factor which is likely to help humanity is the contemporary dissatisfaction that has arisen with materialism, on the one hand, and on the other hand, with spirituality which has been negating the meaning and purposefulness of the material world. After centuries of experiments, materialism is gradually giving way to the pressures of new discoveries which require exploration of the psychical and spiritual domains. Similarly, centuries of experiments in the spiritual fields have shown that the neglect of material life and neglect of collective welfare result in poverty or bankruptcy and even in economic and political slavery. As Sri Aurobindo pointed out :

> "It is therefore of good augury that after many experiments and verbal solutions we should now find ourselves standing today in the presence of the two that

> have alone borne for long the most rigorous tests of experience, the two extremes .... In Europe and in India, respectively, the negation of the materialist and the refusal of the ascetic have sought to assert themselves as the sole truth and to dominate the conception of Life. In India, if the result has been a great heaping up of the treasures of the Spirit, — or of some of them, — it has also been a great bankruptcy of Life; in Europe, the fullness of riches and the triumphant mastery of this world's powers and possessions have progressed towards an equal bankruptcy in the things of the Spirit ...Therefore the time grows ripe and the tendency of the world moves towards a new and comprehensive affirmation in thought and in inner and outer experience and to its corollary, a new and rich self-fulfilment in an integral human existence for the individual and for the race."

It has now become clear that the knowledge of the Spirit and the knowledge of Matter need to be blended and synthesized; supracosmic aim of life has to be enlarged by integrating with it the cosmic aim of life; the realizations of the Spirit have to be extended so as to cover the domain of Matter. And in doing so, all that is intermediate between Spirit and Matter has also to be perfected and brought into unity in complete integration. All this has to be done both at the collective level and a the individual level, and in doing so, we shall find it necessary to develop integral education.

If we analyse the human being, we shall find that between two poles of the body and the spirit, there are three other elements - the vital, the mental and the psychic. We shall again find that all these elements have a constitutional relationship among them; they do not stand in relation of juxtaposition. The physical and the vital can, to a great extent, be controlled and guided by the mental, and up to a certain stage of development, the mind can act as the leader, justifying the description of the mental in the Taittiriya Upanishad, of *manomaya* as *shariraprananeta* (leader of the body and the vital). But the leadership of the mind is rather restricted, and as the rational, ethical and aesthetic powers begin to develop, the mind finds itself incapable of resolving the conflicts between the rational pursuit of truth, aesthetic pursuit of beauty, and ethical pursuit of the good. The mind is found also to be incapable of dealing successfully the forces of Unreason which surge up constantly from the vital and the physical, which, in turn, are greatly dominated by the forces of the subconscious and the unconscious. The time must come when the psychic being, which is called in the Upanishad *antaratman* or which is described in the Vedas as the Mystic Fire (Agni), has to be brought forward as the priest (purohita) of the human journey. And as the psychic being develops, there comes about a powerful opening of the doors of the domains of the spiritual consciousness, which culminate in the supramental, which is called in the Taittiriya Upanishad, *vijnanamaya,* which alone has been found capable of establishing the true integration of all the powers of the being under its natural and spontaneous sovereignty.

The knowledge of the secrets of this entire process of development is largely contained in the Vedas and the Upanishads, and what we find missing there has been discovered and perfected by Sri Aurobindo. It is in the light of all this knowledge that we can speak today with great assurance of the concept and practice of integral education and of the synthesis of the ancient secrets of the reign of Spirit over mind, life and the body and the modern secrets of utilisation of the life in perfecting the instrumentality of the body, life and mind.

Integral education would not only aim at the integral development of personality, but it would also embrace all knowledge in its scope. It would pursue physical and psychical sciences not merely to know the world and Nature in her processes and to use them for material human needs, but to know through them the Spirit in the world and the ways of the Spirit in its appearances. It would study ethics in order, not only to search for the good as the mind sees it, but also to perceive the supra-ethical Good. Similarly, it would pursue Art not merely to present images of the subjective and the objective world, but to see them with significant and creative vision that goes behind their appearances and to reveal the supra-rational Truth and Beauty. It would encourage the study of humanities, not in order to foster a society as a background for a few luminous spiritual figures to that the many necessarily remain for ever on the lower ranges of life, but to inspire the regeneration of the total life of the earth and to encourage voluntary optimism for that regeneration in spite of all previous failures. Finally, it would encourage unity of knowledge and harmony of knowledge, and it would strive to foster the spirit of universality and oneness.

An important characteristic of integral education is its insistence on simultaneous development of Knowledge, Will, Harmony, and Skill as also of all the parts of the being to the extent possible from the earliest stages of education. And since each individual child is unique in the composition of its qualities and characteristics, its capacities and potentialities, its predominant inclinations and propensities, integral education in its practice tends to become increasingly individualized. Again, for this very reason the methods of education become increasingly dynamic, involving active participation of the child in its own growth.

Sri Aurobindo speaks of three principles of teaching, and they all need to be fully implemented in the practice of integral education. Sri Aurobindo states:

> "The first principle of true teaching is that nothing can be taught. The teacher is not an instructor or task master, he is a helper and a guide. His business is to suggest and not to impose. ...The second principle is that the mind has to

> be consulted in its own growth. The idea of hammering the child into the shape desired by the parent or teacher is a barbarous and ignorant superstition. It is he himself who must be induced to expand in accordance with his own nature. ...The chief aim of education should be to help the growing soul to draw out that in itself which is best and make it perfect for a noble use. ...The third principle of education is to work from the near to the far, from that which is to that which shall be. ...A free and natural growth is the condition of genuine development. ..."

These principles, when implemented, provide a basis of a system of a natural organisation of the highest processes and the movements of which the human nature is capable. The first task of the teacher is to *observe* every child and to develop dynamic methods by which the child can be lifted up in its totality into a higher light which can sharpen, chisel, purify, perfect and transform every part of the being in a state of constant balance and integrity. This would mean application of every possible method even to the minutest details and to the action which may seem most insignificant in their appearances with as much care and thoroughness as to the greatest. For there is nothing too small to be used and nothing too great to be attempted.

There are three instruments of the teachers : instruction, example and influence. The good teacher will seek to awaken much more than to instruct; he will aim at the growth of the faculties and the experiences by a natural process and free expansion. He will not impose his opinions on the passive acceptance of the receptive mind; he will throw in only what is productive and sure as a seed which will grow under the benign fostering within. He will know that the example is more powerful than instruction. Actually, the example is not that of the outward acts but of the inner motivation of life and the inner states and inner activities. Finally, influence is more important than example. For influence proceeds from the power or contact of the teacher with his pupil, from the nearness of his soul to the soul of another, infusion into the pupil, even though in silence, all that which the teacher himself is or possesses. The good teacher is himself a constant student. He is a child leading children, and a light kindling other lights, a vessel and a channel.

In our present system of education, we are too occupied with the mental development, and we give a preponderant importance to those qualities which are relevant to subject-oriented, book-oriented and examination-oriented system. We do not give so much importance to the development of powers of understanding as to the powers of memory. We do not emphasize the development of imagination as much as we emphasize the power to knowing facts. We do not give importance to the pursuit of Truth as much as to the pursuit of piece-meal information. Some place is, indeed, being given to physical education and aesthetic education, but these aspects of education are so peripheral that they tend to be almost neglected. In regard to inner domains of personality, the situation is totally unsatisfactory. We sometimes speak of value education, but the situation is so confusing that there is a great need to clarify the entire domain of moral and spiritual values which would also throw considerable light on what we should mean by psychic and spiritual education.

A question is often raised as to whether there is any valid distinction between moral and spiritual values. In answer, it must be said that much depends upon what we intend to include in our definition of the word "morality" or the word "spirituality". In Indian thought, the distinction between morality and spirituality has been clearly made and we have two definite terms, *naitika* and *adhyatimika*, having their specific and distinguishing connotations. The word "morality" connotes a pursuit of the control and mastery over impulses and desires under the guidance and supervening inspiration of a standard of conduct formulated in consideration of man's station and duties in the society or in consideration of any discovered or prescribed intrinsic law of an ideal. Morality is often conceived as a preparation for spirituality. Spirituality, on the other hand, begins when one seeks whatever one conceives to be the ultimate and absolute for its own sake unconditionally and without any reserve whatsoever. Moreover, while morality is often limited to the domains of duties, spirituality is fundamentally a search of the knowledge of the highest and the absolute by direct experience and of manifestation of this knowledge in every mode of feeling, thinking and acting.

Again, what is called religious is distinguishable from the moral and the spiritual. The differentia by which religion can be distinguished from morality and spirituality are : (i) a specific *religious belief;* (ii) certain prescribed acts and rituals and ceremonies, and (iii) a religious authority to which religious matters are referred for final decision.

Both moral and spiritual values can be practised irrespective of whether one believes in one religion or another or whether one believes in no religion. Both morality and spirituality can be independent of rituals and ceremonies or of any acts specifically prescribed by any particular religion, and both of them are independent of any authority except that of direct, abiding and verifiable experience.

Spirituality proceeds directly by change of consciousness, change from the ordinary consciousness to a greater consciousness in which one finds one's true unegoistic being and comes first into direct and living contact and then into union with the Spirit. In spirituality, this change of consciousness is the one thing that matters, nothing else. Both morality and religion in their deepest core touch spirituality and may prepare the change of consciousness, but spirituality not only aims at the total change of consciousness, but even its *method* is that of a gradual and increasing change of consciousness. In other words, spirituality is an exploration of consciousness through progressive change of consciousness.

In the spiritual consciousness, and in the knowledge that it delivers, there is the fulfilment of the highest that morality and religion in their deepest core seek and succeed only when they cease to be limited within their specific boundaries. It replaces the moral law by a progressive law of self-perfection spontaneously expressing itself through the individual nature. No more in this operation is the imposition of a rule or an imperative on the individual nature. The spiritual law respects the individual nature, modifies it and perfects it, and in this sense, it is unique for each individual and can be known and made operative only during the course of the change of consciousness. In its progressive movement, it may, if necessary, provide a short or long period of governance by a moral law, but always as a provisional device and always looking for going beyond into a plane of spontaneous expression of the Right and the Good. To spiritual consciousness, moral virtue is not valuable in itself, but only as an expression of a complex of certain qualities which are, for the time being, for the given individual necessary and useful in an upward journey. For the spiritual consciousness, what is commonly called vice has, too, behind it a complex of certain qualities which have a certain utility in the economy of Nature, and can, therefore, be converted by placing them in their right place, as a complement to what lies in consciousness behind the commonly called virtues.

Spirituality is not confined merely to the aspect of conduct; it includes all works and strives by the method of a progressive change of consciousness for the perfect harmonization of all the aspects of works; and through this striving it realizes also the unity of works with the highest Knowledge and the deepest Love.

For the spiritual consciousness, what is commonly called agnosticism, scepticism, atheism, positivism or free thinking, has behind it a concern and a demand for a direct knowledge, which if rightly understood, recognised, respected and fulfilled, would become a powerful complement to what lies in consciousness behind the commonly accepted religious qualities of faith and unquestioning acceptance of dogmatic teachings and injunctions.

For spirituality always looks behind the form to essence and to the living consciousness; and in doing so, it brings to the surface that which lies behind, and its action is therefore of a new creation. Spirituality transcends the forms and methods of morality and religion and recreates its own living and progressive forms. In the words of Sri Aurobindo:

> "Spirituality is in its essence an awakening to the inner reality of our being, to a spirit, self, soul which is other than our mind, life and body, an inner aspiration to know, to feel, to be that, to enter into contact with the greater Reality beyond and pervading the universe which inhabits also our own being, to be in communion with It and union with I and a turning, a conversion, a transformation of our whole being as a result of the aspiration, the contact, the union, a growth or waking into a new becoming or new being, a new self, a new nature."

Spirituality and spiritual values and the methods of realizing them are distinctive. A mere learning about spirituality is not spirituality; even the most catholic book on spirituality cannot be a substitute for the direct practice of inner change of consciousness by which one can perceive and realize the inner and higher Self and transform the workings of the outer instruments of nature. The education that aims at inculcation of spiritual values and at the synthesis of these values with the dynamic demands of life must be quite radical. It would not do merely to prescribe a few graded books on morality or spirituality and to allot a certain fixed quantities of hours for the study of these books. Spirituality is a living process and spiritual or true education is a process of kindling inner light. Again, spiritual values are central values and they must therefore govern and guide all the values and aspects of education.

In various domains of education, spiritual consciousness can be aided by promoting certain specific values. In the domain of physical education, the values that we ought to promote are those of health, strength, plasticity, grace and beauty. In the domain of vital education, the values that we ought to promote would be those of harmony and friendliness, of courage and heroism, of endurance and perseverance, and the irresistible will to conquer the forces of ignorance, division and injustice. In the domain of mental development, the values that we ought to seek would be those of utmost impartiality, dispassionate search of the Truth, Calm and Silence, and widest possible synthesis. The values pertaining to the aesthetic development would be those of the vision of the Beauty and creative joy of the deepest possible aesthetic experience and expression.

Moreover, life itself is the great teacher of life; therefore, unless spiritual values are the very atmosphere and life- breath of the educational environment, they cannot be truly and effectively brought home to the students.

The pursuit of the spiritual values is, in fact, the pursuit and cultivation of the truths and powers of two over-ruling aspects of personality, namely, what we have called the psychic and the spiritual.

The psychic being is the real individual, the real person behind all personality; it is integrative but unegoistic, and, little by little, it projects itself into the body, life and mind, in proportion to their right development, and suffuses them with its light and purity and establishes by it progressive governance a harmony of the different parts of the being. It is that which knows its real mission as an individual expression in the totality of all the individuals in the world, a mission that is unique to itself. Its goal is a higher realisation upon earth and its law of action is that of mutuality and unity.

While the psychic is the inmost and deepest being in us, the spiritual is the highest and transcendental. While psychic life is the life of immortality and of endless time, and limitless space, the spiritual consciousness, on the other hand, means to live the infinite and eternal, to throw oneself outside all creation beyond time and space.

And there is still a higher ingredient, supramental consciousness, which reconciles the transcendental tendency of the spiritual and the immanence of the psychic as also the powers and perfections of the mental, the vital and the physical.

Integral Education as Life-long Education

Integral education is life-long education, and it beings even before the birth of body and continues throughout the life. And while in the beginning, a great stress falls on the development of the body, life and mind, much can be done both by parents and teachers to commence psychic education at the early stages of development. In fact, the psychic being is very responsive in childhood, and if the right atmosphere is provided to it, and if at the later stages, great care is taken to provide physical, vital and mental education on proper lines, psychic being can be helped to come more and more to the forefront, and discovery of the psychic being can be greatly facilitated. This discovery is considered in integral education as of supreme importance, because through it one becomes conscious of one's destiny and master of one's life.

Psychic Education

In her small but great book on Education, The Mother has stated the following :

> "The psychic being is a great discovery which requires at least as much fortitude and endurance as the discovery of new continents. A few simple words of advice may be useful to one who has resolved to undertake it.
>
> "The first and perhaps the most important point is that the mind is incapable to judging spiritual things. All those who have written on this subject have said so; but very few are those who have put it into practice. And yet, in order to proceed on the path, it is absolutely indispensable to abstain from all mental opinion and reaction.
>
> "Give up all personal seeking for comfort, satisfaction, enjoyment or happiness. Be only a burning fire for progress, take whatever comes to you as an aid to your progress and immediately make whatever progress is required.
>
> "Try to take pleasure in all you do, but never do anything for the sake of pleasure.
>
> "Never get excited, nervous or agitated. Remain perfectly calm in the face of all circumstances. And yet be always alert to discover what progress you still have to make and lose no time in making it.
>
> "Never take physical happenings at their face value, they are always a clumsy attempt to express something else, the true thing which escapes our superficial understanding.
>
> "Never complain of the behavior of anyone, unless you have the power to change in his nature what makes him

act in this way; and if you have the power, change him instead of complaining.

"Whatever you do, never forget the goal which you have set before you. There is nothing great or small once you have set out on this great discovery; all things are equally important and can either hasten or delay its success. Thus before you eat, concentrate a few seconds in the aspiration that the food you are about to eat may bring your body the substance it needs to serve as a solid basis for your effort towards the great discovery, and give it the energy for persistence and perseverance in the effort.

"Before you go to sleep, concentrate a few seconds in the aspiration that the sleep may restore your fatigued nerves; bring calm and quiteness to your brain so that on waking you may, with renewed vigor, begin again your journey on the path of the great discovery.

"Before you act, concentrate in the will that your action may help or at least in no way hinder your march forward towards the great discovery.

"When you speak, before the words come out of your mouth, concentrate just long enough to check your words and allow only those that are absolutely necessary to pass, only those that are not in any way harmful to your progress on the path of the great discovery.

"To sum up, never forget the purpose and goal of your life. The will for the great discovery should be always there above you, above what you do and what you are, like a huge bird of light dominating all the movements of your being."

As far as the aid that parents and teachers can give, it may first be noted that a good many children are under the influence of the psychic presence which shows itself very distinctively at times in their spontaneous reactions and even in their words. All spontaneous turning to love, truth, beauty, knowledge, nobility, heroism, is a sure sign of the psychic influence. To recognize these reactions and to encourage them wisely and with a psychic feeling would be the first indispensable step.

It is also important to note that to say good words, to give wise advice to a child has very little effect, if one does not show by one's living example the truth of what one teaches.

The best qualities to develop in children are sincerity, honesty, straightforwardness, courage, disinterestedness, unselfishness, patience, endurance, perseverance, peace, calm and self-control, and they are taught infinitely better by example than by speeches, however, beautiful.

The role of the teacher is to put the child upon the right road to his own perfection and encourage him to follow it watching, suggesting, helping, but not imposing or interfering. The best method of suggestion is by personal example, daily conversation, and books read from day-to-day.

These books should contain, for younger students, the loftiest examples of the past, given not as moral lessons but as things of supreme human interest, and for elder students, the great thoughts of great souls, the passages of literature which can set fire to the highest emotions and prompt the highest ideals and aspirations, the records of history and biography which exemplify the living of those great thoughts, noble emotions and inspiring ideals.

Opportunity should be given to students to emulate in action the deeper and nobler impulses which rise within them.

The undesirable impulses and habits should not be treated harshly. The child should not be scolded except with a definite purpose and only when it is felt indispensable. Particularly, care should be taken not to rebuke the child for a fault which one commits oneself. Children are very keen and clear-sighted observers; they take no time to find out the weaknesses and note them without pity.

When a child makes a mistake, one must see that he confesses it to the teacher or the guardian spontaneously and frankly; and when the has confessed, he should be made to understand with kindness and affection what was wrong in the movement and precaution should be taken to see that he does not repeat it. A fault confessed must be forgiven. The child should be encouraged to think of wrong impulses not as sins or offences but as symptoms of a curable disease, alterable by a steady and sustained effort of the will, — falsehood being rejected and replaced by truth, fear by courage, selfishness by sacrifice, attachment by renunciation and malice by love.

Due care should be taken to see that unformed virtues are not rejected as faults. The wildness and recklessness of many young natures are only the overflowing of excessive strength, greatness and nobility. They should be purified and not discouraged.

Affection that sees clearly, is firm and yet gentle and a sufficiently practical knowledge will create bonds of trust that are indispensable for the educator to make education of the child effective.

When a child asks a question, he should not be answered by saying that it is stupid or foolish, or that the answer will not be understood by him. Curiosity cannot be postponed, and effort should be made to answer the question truthfully and in such a way as to make the answer accessible to the brain of the hearer.

With the growing awareness, the child should be taught to concentrate on the inner psychic presence and make it more and more a living reality.

The child should be taught that whenever there is an inner uneasiness, he should not pass it off and try to forget it, but should attend to it and try to find out by an inner observation and cause of the uneasiness so that it may be removed by some methods, inner or outer.

When the psychic being begins to be discovered, we find that it burns in the temple of the inmost heart behind the thick screen of the ignorant mind, life and body. As Sri Aurobindo points out :

> "The veiled psychic is the flame of the Godhead always alight within us, inextinguishable even by that dense unconsciousness of any spiritual self within which obscures our outward nature...It is the concealed Witness and Control, the hidden Guide, the Daemon of Socrates, the inner light or inner voice of the mystic ...It is the individual soul, Caitya Purusa, supporting mind, life and body, standing behind the mental, the vital, the subtle-physical being in us and watching and profiting by their development and experience...It is this secret psychic entity which is the true original Conscience in us deeper than the constructed and conventional conscience of the moralist, for it is this which points always towards Truth and Right and Beauty, towards Love and Harmony and all that is a divine possibility in us, and persists till these things become the major need of our nature...If the secret psychic person can come forward into the front...the whole nature can be turned towards the real aim of life, the supreme victory, the ascent into spiritual existence."

Mental Education

In regard to mental education, the processes and methods can best be determined by understanding of the mind. Mind is concerned largely with the activities of understanding, and all understanding is a discovery of a centre around which the ideas or things in question are held together.

Mental education is a process of training the mind of students to arrive at such central conceptions around which the widest and most complex and subtle ideas can be assimilated and integrated.

It is again found that even these central conceptions point still to a beyond, to their own essential Meaning, which can be glimpsed and conceived by the mind, but which cannot be held and possessed fully in experience by the mind. This point marks the climax of the mental development as also a clear sign of the limitations of the mind. Having reached there its office is to fall into contemplation of silence and to open to the higher realms of experience, to receive clearly and precisely the institutions and inspirations from those higher realms, and to give creative expression to them.

To train the mind on these lines, there are five phases of the programme :

— Development of the power of concentration, and attention;

— Development of the capacities of expansion, wideness, complexity and richness;

— Organisation of ideas round a central or a higher ideal or a supremely luminous idea that will serve as a guide in life;

— Thought control, rejection of undesirable thoughts so that one may, in the end, think only what one wants and when one wants;

— Development of mental silence, perfect calm and a more and more total receptivity to inspirations coming from the higher regions of the being.

Multiplicity of ideas, richness of ideas, totality of points of view – these should be made to grow by a developed power of observation and concentration and by a wideness of interests. Care should be taken to see that the central ideas are not imposed upon the growing mind – that would be the dogmatic method, which tends to atrophy the mind. The mind should grow towards central ideas which should come as a discovery of the mind made through rigorous exercise of the rational faculty.

Stress should fall not only on understanding, but also on criticism and control of ideas; not only on comprehension, synthesis, creativity, judgement, imagination, memory and observation, but also on critical functions of comparison, reasoning, deduction, inference and conclusion. Both these aspects of human reason are essential to the completeness of the mental training.

One of the best methods is to create an atmosphere in which massive and powerful ideas are constantly thrown as a stimulation and challenge impelling the students to arrive at them or strive to grasp and assimilate them.

Thinkers alone can produce thinkers; and unless teachers are constantly in the process of building up great thoughts and ideas, it is futile to expect a sound or vigorous mental education.

An atmosphere vibrant at once with ideation and silence, an atmosphere surcharged with synthetic thoughts and most integral aspirations and an atmosphere filled with the widest realisation and a harmonious unity – such an atmosphere is indispensable for perfect mental education.

A constant attempt should be made to present each topic to the student in a challenging way so as to stimulate him and create his interest in the topic. To find new and imaginative methods, to compile materials from various sources, to introduce new concepts and new interpretations in various subjects, to develop new subjects, and above all, to attend in detail to all the psychological faculties and their development in such a way that the mental education does not veil the soul — this, in brief, should be the endeavour and its spirit.

Vital Education

Vital education aims at training the life-force (that normally vibrates in emotions, desires and impulses) in three directions: to discover its real function and to replace its egoistic and ignorant tendency so as to become the master by a willingness and capacity to serve higher principles of the psychological constitution; to subtilise and sublimate its sensitivity which expresses itself through sensuous and aesthetic activities; and to resolve and transcend the dualities and contradictions in the character constituted by the vital seekings, and to achieve the transformation of the character.

The usual methods of dealing with the vital have been those of coercion, suppression, abstinence and asceticism. But these methods do not give lasting results. Besides, they only help in drying up the drive and dynamism of the life-force; and thus the collaboration of the life-force in self-fulfilment is eliminated.

The right training of the vital then is much more subtle and much more difficult, needing endurance, endless persistence and an inflexible will. For what is to be aimed at is not the negation of life but the fulfilment of life by its transformation.

First, the powers of the senses have to be developed, subtilised and enriched. Next, there are inner and latent senses which are to be discovered and similarly developed. Third, the seekings of these senses have to be trained to reject grossness and coarseness and to enjoy the finer tastes and higher aesthetic experiences. Finally, there has to be a deeper and piercing observation of the desires, passions, ambitions, lusts, etc., their risings, revolts and contradictions, and an attempt by various methods of separate but in each movement the elements that contribute to the concord and harmony from those tending in the opposite direction, and to eliminate these latter from the very nature and fibre of our psychological constitution.

The effective methods of this last aspect are :-

— to instill in the child, as soon as possible, the will towards progress and perfection ;

— rational arguments, sentiment and goodwill, or appeal to the sense of dignity and self-respect, according to the nature of the child in question;

— to insist on the idea that the will can be developed, and that no defeat should be taken as final;

— to demand from the will the maximum effort, for the will is strengthened by effort;

— above all, the example of the educator shown constantly and sincerely.

But still the direction in which the effort has to be made can be known only by the training of the mind and by the opening of the secret knowledge that is within our psychic being. To develop therefore in the vital the habit to open to this light and to act in that light would be to place the vital in its proper place as a will-force executing the inner and higher knowledge.

Vital education is greatly aided by stress on different kinds of fine arts and crafts. Sri Aurobindo has written at length on the contribution that Art can make to the integral education in his important book, *"The National Value of Art"*. He has pointed out that the first and the lowest use of Art is the purely aesthetic, the second is the intellectual and the third and the highest is the spiritual. He has even stated that music, art and poetry are a perfect education for the soul; they make and keep its movement purified, deep and harmonious. He has added,

> "These, therefore, are agents which cannot profitably be neglected by humanity on its onward march or degraded to the mere satisfaction of sensuous pleasure which will disintegrate rather than build the character. They are, when properly used, great educating, edifying the civilizing forces."

A great lesson in vital education is to develop the will of the individual and to encourage the exercise of the will in which what is valued most is not the result, but application and doing one's best.

Physical Education

On the subject of physical education, it must be mentioned that the physical is our base, and even the highest spiritual values are to be expressed through the life that is embodied here. *Sariram adyam khalu dharmasadhanam,* says the old Sanskrit adage, — the body is the means of fulfilment of dharma, while *dharma* means every ideal which we can propose to ourselves and the law of its working out and its action.

Of all the domains of education, physical is the one most completely governed by method, order, discipline and procedure. All education of the body must be rigorous, detailed and methodical.

The education of the body has three principal aspects: control and discipline of functions of the body; a total methodical and harmonious development of all the parts and movements of the body; rectification of defects and deformities, if there are any.

Physical education must be based upon knowledge of the human body, its structure and its functions. And the formation of the habits of the body must be in consonance with that knowledge.

The child should be taught right from the early stage the right positions, postures and movements.

A similar training should be with regard to the choice of food. The child should develop the taste that is simple and healthy, substantial and appetising. He must avoid all that merely stuffs and causes heaviness; particularly, he must be taught to eat according to his hunger and not make food a means to satisfy his greed and gluttony.

The child should also be taught the taste for cleanliness and hygienic habits. It is important to impress upon the child that he is not more interesting by being ill, rather the contrary. Children should be taught that to be ill is a sign of failing and inferiority, not of virtue or sacrifice.

Freedom and Discipline

A very important problem in respect of integral education arises from its insistence on proper synthesis between freedom and discipline. Since education is a creative process, and since compulsion and creativity cannot go together, freedom has to be a very important instrument of education. The ideal condition is obtained when discipline becomes the child of freedom and discipline is transformed into self-discipline.

We have to recognise that different children react to various activities of education differently. There are children who feel a powerful attraction towards creative activities such as arts, music, dance, composition of poetry, drama, etc. They should, of course, be given freedom to pursue these valuable activities. But there are instances where children who do not have this natural inclination towards creative activities are also compelled to be engaged in these activities. This is entirely unacceptable.

We may also need to note that there are children who do not easily respond either to the activities of creativity or activities of production, but who are deeply reflective and to whom abstraction of thought and clarity and beauty of ideation constitute a fascinating project. We must recognise that a deep exercise in ideation and organisation of ideas is a very active engagement. It is a great activity of concentration.

At the same time, an exclusive pursuit of ideation without devoting any attention whatever to creative or productive activity may lead to a lopsided development of personality. But the remedy is not to make things compulsory, but to counsel children, to motivate and suggest to them how gradually various kinds of activities can be blended together for a harmonious development. But while counselling, the teacher must realise and appreciate that there are periods where psychologically even an exclusive development of ideate activity or productive activity or creative activity has its legitimate claims. To what degree this claim has to be satisfied and in what way this claim has to be subordinated to the other claims of development will demand from the teacher a very deep insight into the inner psychological workings of the formation of the personality and his sympathetic understanding of the psychological differences among various children.

It may also be noted that there are children who are deeply interested in activities of self-sacrifice or of purifying their base emotions, or of the worship of the noblest ideals of life. Sometimes they may show no interest in studies or in arts or in crafts and often teachers complain of their dullness or their lack of concentration in studies. But a good teacher should ask himself if the child in question is not inwardly engaged in what may be called activities of "purification".

There could also be children like Yuddishthira who would not claim that they have learnt a lesson unless they have succeeded in practising it in their daily life. These are indeed noble children and the teacher should be able to appreciate their nobility and encourage it so as to lead it to its perfection.

During the course of educational process, students often come up with some very fundamental questions but they often remain unanswered. Why, for example, should one learn mathematics? What does really history teach us? What is the relationship between language and mathematics? What is the aim of life? There should be freedom to raise these questions and also enough time and readiness to answer them, even though they may not be a part of any prescribed syllabus.

Another important point that should be noted is that a great care should be taken to get the development of the child in such a way that inspite of the growth of knowledge, the student does not lose freshness and sense of wonder and mystery. This indeed is the most difficult part of the work of the teacher.

6

Teaching Integral Education

An Integrated Model Framework

The new model will be so flexible that it can accommodate or adjust itself with the various programmes of education of varying durations. In particular, this model will aim at providing the necessary structure and organisation so as to permit the art of self-learning and integral development of personality as also various combinations of programmes of agricultural, technical, vocational, artistic and academic education. It will also facilitate the creation of the atmosphere and stimulation needed for dynamic methods. Besides, it will also meet the needs of multi-point entry system, non-formal education, part-time education, and of weaving examination system into the learning process itself.

Grouping of Students

For each major stage of studies (lower primary, higher primary, etc.) there could normally be sections or groups of about 100 students. The differences of levels of capacities should not very much count in the formation of these large groupings. These groupings would be valid and useful for those areas of studies which yield easily to cooperative work, mass media or to the means of environmental influence. These would include works of productive labour, large portions of language-learning, as also introductory or panoramic portions of a number of subjects where demonstrations, exhibitions or stimulating and interesting lectures and suitable means of communication. These would also be relevant to what may be regarded as peripheral areas of studies, where the imparting of general information is intended. Areas of general explanations, general knowledge, general instructions are also appropriate to these large groupings.

In the general working of the organisations, it is better not to have any fixed time-table for the work of these large groupings. Or, if it is found necessary for some reason to have a regular fixed timing, it is better to have it not for the main work but to confine it to what may be termed 'time for supplementary work'.

In any case, the fixed timings of various programmes of education should be so arranged that the hours of fresh study and labour which can be done by individual self-learning are not affected in any way.

For purposes of the individual self-learning, there will be, in a sense, no groupings since each individual will be free to choose his own area of work and pursue it at his own pace.

(a) But each teacher will have a number of students who will come to him more or less regularly for consultation on the subject of his competence. These students would, in a sense, constitute for the teacher in question a kind of a natural group. For, although these students will mostly come individually for consultations, they might also come in the form of a group from time to time.

(b) There will be, however, another kind of grouping or break-up of the large group, depending upon the mode of learning that a given topic imposes or upon the mode of learning chosen by the student There are topics or areas which need to be pursued regularly, systematically, step by step, with rigour, measure and regulated or accelerated speed. Those who choose such topics or such a mode of learning will form a kind of a group-even though each of them may do his work mostly by himself. There are other areas or topics, which may permit a leisurely and free pursuit. Those who choose such topics or such a mode of learning will from another group. These groupings will, however, be not tight and inflexible. The same student may belong to one group for a few topics and to another group for other topics; or, with regard to the same topic, he may offer to do both these kinds of work appropriate to both these groups. Thus, he will belong to both the groups.

It may be noted that the grouping mentioned above under (a) and (b) will be, more or less, temporary, meant for some specific purpose or project and therefore dissoluble with the purpose in view. These groups will normally tend to be homogeneous from the point of view of capacities, or interests, but these will often need to have group classes, and sometimes, even a fixed time-table for short or long periods. Normally, time-tables should be fixed for a month or two, renewable for a longer period, if necessary.

Individual consultations with the teachers will also tend in the direction of regular prior fixation of timings in regard to each student. There' are some obvious advantages and conveniences in such fixed appointments. But care should be taken to see that the teachers keep always one or two hours daily unfixed so that students may have the opportunity to come to them from time to time without any prior engagement.

One final point about grouping. If we are watchful, we shall find that, from time to time, there emerge spontaneously extremely small groups of students who have common inclinations of high aspirations, some common character or common trait of personality, even though they may differ in respect of capacities. Their homogeneity is by virtue of character or personality rather than capacities. Such groups are very valuable. They should be recognised, and they should be given all the help needed individually or collectively. Such groups become, if properly encouraged, transmitters of enthusiasm, dedication and devotion to studies, work and ideas.

In regard to the above system of grouping, three obvious advantages can be mentioned:

(1) There has recently been a strong plea for multi-point entry system, particularly, in relation to the solutions which have been suggested for the implementation of the programme for the universalisation of elementary education. It will be noted that this idea of multi-point entry system is extremely valuable, and this system will find a natural setting in the structure that is suggested here. Similarly, this structure will provide a favourable setting for 'unit' studies. And a new system of tests can easily operate in the proposed structure so that tests become a part of the natural rhythm of the process of learning.

(2) It would be possible in this flexible organisation to ensure facilities for individual attention which is indispensable, particularly, in the field of moral and spiritual education.

(3) Works of productive labour can flourish in this setting with naturalness that is so essential to the joy of work. These works needs not be given as tasks. But students can be stimulated and encouraged by

means of nourishment of interests, environmental needs and influences, as also through the medium of hobbies. In this setting, even specialisation of vocational training can be initiated at early stages. General education, diversification of courses and vocationalisation - all can blend harmoniously together.

Teachers

(a) The role of teachers in this new organisation is crucial. The teachers should have not only competence with regard to their subjects but also the necessary spirit and zeal.

(b) In the initial stages, students will need to learn how to organise their freedom; teachers should, therefore, help students in this regard.

(c) For every unit of 100 students, there should be a Coordinator or a 'First Teacher' whose functions will be as follows:

   (i) He will be available to students for guidance so as to help them in organising their work and in learning the art of self-learning as also other ways of learning;

   (ii) He may, by personal contact, provide motivation to the students for various works, topics or subjects, accordings to the needs and circumstances;

   (iii) he will ensure that all the material needs of studies and work are provided for;

   (iv) He will keep an overall record of the work of every student in the unit, and will see that the students get the necessary guidance from himself or from the other teachers, or else from the environment;

(v) He will also ensure that the entire organisation runs smoothly and harmoniously;

(vi) He will work as a brother among brothers and will consult all concerned before arriving at decisions; and

(vii) He will also give the necessary help in framing time-table, particularly, in view of the fact that, since there will be no time-tables fixed in advance for the whole year, there will be the need to frame *ad hoc* time-tables for short or long durations in consultation with students and teachers for various subjects and for various purposes.

(d) In addition to the First Teachers, it seems practicable that, for each major subject, a full-time competent teacher could take charge of about 30-40 students (this number may vary according to the special needs of a given subject and also the age and capacity of the students). These teachers may form themselves into a small committee to help the Coordinator, and maintain a personal contact with the students in the Unit.

(e) Problems of irregularity, indiscipline and misuse of facilities will primarily be dealt with by the Coordinator and his Committee. To this Committee may be nominated some of the best students of the Unit.

(f) All administrative problems should be handled carefully so that all points of view are given their due weight, and decisions emerge out of consultations.

(g) All work should be carried out by utmost goodwill and cooperative action, rather than by any arbitrary authority.

(h) There should be no place for gossips, politics, canvassing, maneuvering, ugliness and untidiness. There should be an atmosphere of self-control and utmost inner discipline.

(i) A full-fledged working of this model will presuppose new educational material in the form of booklets, work-sheets, charts, maps, pictures, albums, tapes, slides, film-strips, magazines, journals, exhibits, tools, and equipment and apparatus. And new curricula and syllabi have to be worked out, particularly, in regard to interdisciplinary studies and interweaving of work and knowledge. In these tasks, teachers will have to make their own contribution.

Organisation of the Work

In the proposed organisation, a special emphasis will fall upon 'individual work'. 'Individual Work' may be pursued in several different ways that have already been enumerated elsewhere.

At the end of every two or three months, each student will submit to the Coordinator a report on his work in regard to each topic, subject or work under study. This report will give details of the progress he has made in regard to what he has read or written or the reflections and conclusions he has arrived at.

Tests will be given to the students where necessary, and their aim will be to provide to the students occasions for exercise, revision, comprehension, encouragement and self-evaluation.

Tests for placement in the employment market should be conducted by a National Testing Service, and they should be open to anyone who wants to take them. These tests should be related to specific jobs or employment opportunities or certain pursuits of studies and disciplines of knowledge and skill.. They will also test physical fitness, and other talent, practical skills and value orientation.

What will be Expected of Students

To learn the secret of self-education and to work hard so as to remain steadily on the road to self-perfection - this will be the student's constant endeavour.

To study and work widely and intensely, to study and work with joy and application, to study and work to grow and to remain perpetually youthful-this will be the content of his main work.

But to become a fearless hero-warrior in the quest of Truth, Harmony, and Liberty, and to surpass the limitations of his nature by an inner change and transformation - this will be regarded as the very heart of his work.

CONTENTS OF EDUCATION

Aims of education determine the contents and methods of education. If our aim is that of life-long integral education, the contents of education have to be conceived quite differently from what are normally pursued in our present system of education.

In India, almost all schools follow a curriculum which was originally designed to arrive at the end of the educational process within a limited period and to fashion clerical abilities among students. Gradually, it has been expanded to suit the needs of producing lawyers, engineers, medical doctors, businessmen and teachers. Vocational courses have only been recently introduced, even through they have not flourished to any expected degree. Moreover, curricula are so designed that they do not cater to the needs of those who want to or are required to drop out of school system at early .stages. Even the curriculum of class X, which is the first termirtal point in our Indian system, is geared to the needs of higher levels of education. Upto class X, all prescribed studies are compulsory for everybody. Hence, no child can have an experience of free choice and free joy of learning until the completion of class X.

If a student wants to become a mason or a carpenter, our schools have nothing to offer to him. Similarly, if he wants to be a poet, there is hardly anything which would be directly related in our curriculum which would nourish his abilities to become even a budding poet. If one wants to be musician, the student will hardly find anything in his curriculum excepting a few classes in music meant as a part of general education. Examples of this kind can be multiplied.

Let us take the example of physical education, which has somehow secured some place in recent decades in our system of education. There are periods allotted to physical training or to Yoga classes. But what exactly is physical education, what is the importance of the human body, how miraculously human body works, what are different forms of physical education, - these and allied questions receive hardly any place in the curriculum. Something about the human body is, of course, taught in courses relating to physiology and hygiene, but the orientation is not related to physical education.

Moreover, we find that there are a number of interesting questions and studies which come up if we allow freedom of enquiry and freedom of pursuit of subjects of interest. Students often ask questions like this: "What is below the waters of the ocean?" "What kinds of animals live in the ocean?" "What has been the history of costumes?" "What has been the history of weapons?" "How to learn?" "How to widen interest?" " How to concentrate?" These and allied questions are hardly answered because they do not form part of curriculum or syllabus.

A very important question is being debated in regard to value education. Should there be a special curriculum for this subject? Or else, should the study of values be integrated in different studies? The debate has been inconclusive, and in the meantime, no serious effort has been made to spell out the curriculum in respect of value education.

In regard to the study of languages, curricula do not manifest any concern for developing adequate competence to express oneself faultlessly, perfectly, and beautifully. Where more than one languages are taught, there is no concern to correlate these languages and to advance the capacity of translating from one language to the other. In fact, there are no courses on translations in our schools or in colleges.

In one of his essays of national system of education, Sri Aurobindo had underlined the importance of language in the development of mental faculties. He had said that mental faculty should first be exercised on things, afterwards on words and ideas. But he had added, "Our dealings with language are much too perfunctory and absence of fine sense for words impoverishes the intellect and limits the fineness and truth of its operation. The mind should be accustomed first to notice the word thoroughly, its form, sound and sense; then to compare the form with other similar forms in the points of similarity and difference, thus forming the foundation of the grammatical sense; then to distinguish between the fine shades of sense of similar words and the formation and rhythm of different sentences, thus forming the formation of the literary and the syntactical faculties. All this should be done informally, drawing on the curiosity and interest, avoiding set teaching and memorising of rules. The true knowledge takes its base on things, arthas, and only when it has mastered the things, proceeds to formalise its information".

If these ideas of dealings with language have to be fulfilled, we have to think both of new contents and new methods of teaching languages.

The field of history needs a very special attention. It is not sufficiently realised that Indian history, with its uninterrupted continuity of more than five thousand years, has a rich account to be conveyed to students Excepting China, no other country has had such a long historical account, and even in regard to China, the continuity is not so great as in the case of India. As compared to the students in other countries, the Indian students have, therefore, to be obliged to receive and assimilate a much greater burden not only of the quantity of information but also of the complexity of numerous currents of civilisation and culture which had again landmarks of various kinds, the interpretations of which are varied and numerous.

The history books which are now used in our educational system were written during the British period, and they have only been slightly modified during the last fifty years. The question as to how we must present Indian history to Indian students poses many problems, and they have not received the attention that they deserve. Very often, the history of northern India over-shadows the history of southern India; the accounts of various dynasties that ruled parts of India at different times overshadow the accounts of civilisation and culture that developed in various forms in various parts in the country, retaining yet some kind of essential unity; much of the cultural ethos is treated marginally by proclaiming that the concerned literature is legendary or mythological in character; even the basic facts of the most important texts of the ancient Indian history - and for that matter of world history, - namely, of the Vedas, are not known even to the most educated Indians of today; the sheer poetic excellence of the Vedas should have merited the full attention of the whole nation; even the three great national poets of Indian history, Valmiki, Vyasa and Kalidasa, and their works are hardly known and only very briefly mentioned in our history books; the great achievements which were registered by ancient Indians in the fields of astronomy, mathematics, natural sciences, metallurgy, as also in the fields of grammar, ethics, philosophy, religion, psychic and spiritual sciences, yoga, art, music, dance, and architecture, hardly figure in our history books. Even the political account of Indian history suffers from great short-comings and Indian students remain ignorant of how Indian polity developed through the ages and what great dreams and deeds were nurtured by the leading personalities of the country in different epochs.

Again, Indian history is taught in such a way that while a student becomes conversant with, say, Maratha period, he remains quite unacquainted with the Mughal period or earlier periods or subsequent periods. Inter-connections of history are hardly presented or grasped.

It is true that many important facts about India's development are besieged by controversies in regard to their historical accuracies; it is also true that much is not known about many great men and women who flourished in different epochs of history; it is also true that the meanings of some of the greatest products of Indian literature have been interpreted differently by different scholars. But the answer to these questions is to undertake a programme of thorough-going research instead of subjecting them to neglect or even oblivion.

Our students deserve to be given a rich account of the heritage to which they have a natural right.

The question of the study of history is further complicated by the fact that, in order to keep abreast with the increasing drift towards human unity, which is spreading all over the world, we have to teach our students the entire history of the world in a meaningful manner. This subject is very vast, but at this stage, we need not enter into any further details. We may only make a remark that there is a need to present world history and its relationships with Indian history at least in three forms: in synoptic form, in the form of an outline, and in the form of detailed exposition, so that they can suit the needs of atleast three categories of students, namely, those who want to have a general and rapid view, those who want to be acquainted, and those who want to study at a deeper or scholarly level.

Before we leave the subject of history, we may make a few important remarks which are associated with this subject. The first is in connection with the study of legends and mythologies. At one time, there was a great prejudice against ancient beliefs, their symbolism, and their literature which lacked scientific or philosophic rigour. This prejudice is gradually being corrected, and there is today a salutary movement to understand ancient legends and mythologies with fresh eyes. It seems, therefore, desirable that a study of legends and mythologies in so far as they constitute a part of the cultural ethos, should be brought to the notice of our young generations. In any case, our students should not have wrong facts about legends and mythologies.

Accuracy of information on this subject is very important. Secondly, we have deplorable dearth of good biographies of great men and women of our country; a similar deficiency is not there in regard to world history, but our own knowledge of books concerning the same is very limited, and even that limited knowledge does not find any route of transmission to our teachers and students. This is a very important subject, and we must give considerable place to biographies, and accounts of important events should from a part of the contents of education.

Thirdly, we have to take a great care to ensure that the study of the past and the present does not become a prison preventing the visions of the future. There are golden reaches of our consciousness, and from them and from the reaches between them and our ordinary mental consciousness there have descended forces and forms which have become embodied in literature, philosophy, science, in music, drama, art, architecture, sculpture, in great and heroic deeds and in all that is wonderful and precious in the different organised or as yet unorganised aspects of life. To put students in contact with these, Eastern and Western, ancient and present, would be to provide them with the air and atmosphere in which they can breathe an inspiration to reach again to those peaks of consciousness and to create still newer forms and forces which would bring the golden day nearer - this should be the aim of the study of history.

A very important area that is developing today is that of inter-disciplinary studies. At present, this is pursued only at the higher level of education or at the level of research. But there is an urgent need to develop this subject even at lower levels of education. Basically, all subjects are complementary to each other; and there is no subject which is not interesting, provided we can show the interrelationship, of a subject with those subjects which are supposed to be interesting. Many may not know how much mathematics is connected with music, and how Pythagoras saw the relationship between these two subjects; and many do not know or appreciate the relationship between music and poetry.

Again, mathematics is closely connected with logic, - there is even a view that mathematics and logic are one and the same and logic is often considered to be the key of metaphysics; there is an obvious connection between metaphysics and physics; and physics, chemistry and biology are closely interconnected ; again, the main theme of biology is that of evolution, and evolution is closely related to the theme of man. Now, the study of man leads us to the study of history and geography; study of geography leads to the study of the earth, and the study of earth is connected with the study of planets and stars and galaxies and of the entire universe.

In fact, it must be said that the pursuit of man to know himself and the universe and to relate himself with the universe as effectively and harmoniously as possible is the underlying idea of all education. This interrelationship of man and the universe is central to the aim of integral education. If integral education is concerned with the development of the physical, vital, mental, psychic and spiritual parts of the human being, it is also connected with the knowledge that links universal Matter with universal Spirit. And this covers the entire gamut of knowledge and the means by which all knowledge can be united in one unity.

Closely connected with the problem of unity of knowledge is the contemporary problem of explosion of knowledge. Considering this unprecedented explosion, one is obliged to ask as to how one can relate oneself to this explosion in such a way that one is not crushed under the increasing flow of information On the one hand, there is a pressure towards specialisation; on the other hand, there is a pressure for inter-disciplinary and holistic knowledge. Knowing more and more about less and less bestows upon the individual a specialised capacity and proficiency but it also creates disabling inefficiencies in respect of larger questions where multi-sided knowledge is indispensable.

There is more to perplex us. Specialised knowledge and efficiency that the individual possesses today tend to become obsolete at a rapid rate. There is, consequently, increasing pressure to continue to learn all the time. But this leaves very little time to expand horizons in fields other than those of specialisation. With the passage of time, our inefficiency to deal with general questions of life goes on increasing.

At a certain state, this situation, if not corrected, can really become alarming. Crises of various kinds are bound to multiply and this is what we witness today all over the world.

Against this background, an important question that can be raised is whether there is something like "essential knowledge" which every human being, as a human being, ought to possess and which ought to be communicated to every student during the educational career.

Reflecting on this question, it seems that there are at least three global subjects which can be considered to be essential and at the same time inherently inter-disciplinary; if they could be taken up as the basic umbrella of curriculum, we can more easily combine the needs of general and specialised education. The first subject is that of man and the environment, the second subject, which is closely related to the first, is that of man and evolution; and the third subject is that of the aim of life.

As these areas are quite neglected, they acquire special consideration of educationists. Two final remarks need to be made. We find that most of the books which are prescribed in schools and colleges are so written that they are extremely uninteresting. Students read them because they want to pass examinations, and often they take to short-cuts and resort to guide books which are even more boring and less instructive. There is a need to prepare learning materials in such a way that every subject is made interesting, vivid and even charming. It may be said that this is a tall order, but when we are thinking not of narrow or immediate goals, and when we are thinking of education for tomorrow, we need not hesitate to make tall orders.

Secondary, if integral education is to be freed from the evils of subject-oriented, book-oriented and examination-oriented system of education, if liberty and self-discipline are to be the hallmark of the methods of integral education, and if the emphasis is to be laid on self-education, we shall need to write books in different forms that will be required for different kinds of students, different kinds of backgrounds and different modes of learning. We have to think of preparing worksheets, workbooks, monographs, reference books, documentation books, and books which can be read along with TV or audio-tapes.

7

Education for Character Development

India is today sinking under the weight of problems, some of which, like those of violence, division, corruption and plutocracy are proving to be most obstinate and most difficult to resolve. We are trying to find solutions but there seem to be certain tendencies and factors which require remedies at a level that is far deeper than the level at which we are now thinking and acting.

At present, we are engrossed within narrow boundaries, and what we lack most is perception of perspectives. We want democracy, but narrowed down in our adoption of the Western form of parliamentary democracy, we do not go to the root of the truth of democracy, namely, the development of the individual to grow into his/her highest possibilities, physical, vital, mental, aesthetic, ethical and spiritual. True democracy demands self-determination by the individual and the collection at the highest levels of consciousness. This demand is consistently and systematically ignored or obstructed, and therefore, democracy is being increasingly collapsing in plutocracy, -the rule of money, the rule of crime and rule of muscle power. Our Constitution speaks of socialism, but we are not adequately cognisant of the way in which socialism tends to grow into deification of the State. As a result, we are not working consciously for the development of collective consciousness that takes care of the liberties of the individual nor are we developing the ethos in which the individual and the collectivity are prepared to sacrifice their egoisms for their harmonious and inter-dependent relationships.

The only way by which we are reducing the impact of socialism is by reviving the grip of capitalism in the name of liberalisation and globalisation. We are not inquiring as to how we can devise means and methods by which, consistent with individual liberty, we can also bring about welfare not merely of a few but of all. Our Constitution also speaks of secularism, but while we easily yield to the tendency to equate secularism with materialism, we do not strain ourselves to transcend the limitations of consciousness where exclusivism of religions is over passed so as to create a dynamic Dharma and dynamic spirituality, which does not shun material life but transforms it for the highest possible synthesis of Spirit and Matter.

We want rapid social transformation, but we are still nourishing those institutions that foster casteism and narrow loyalties. We want rapid economic growth, but confine ourselves to the stifling attitudes, and thus we are unable to inspire adequate individual and collective initiative or required generosity and nobility in our institutions of commerce and industry. While we need sustained effort for development, we are riddled with fluctuations in regard to our priorities. We do think sometimes of education as of highest importance but we remain restricted merely to multiplying the number of educational institutions which continuously increase the impact of Macaulayan ideology of education instead of making bold efforts to transform the objectives, contents and methods of education that will educate all and educate them for development of wisdom and character. In this situation, it has become imperative to underline that the most important theme of India today is that of education for character development.

This theme is also reinforced when we consider not only the Indian situation but the global situation which is constantly influencing and shaping our Indian situation. A huge structure is being built up with an increasing insistence on mechanisation, standardisation and dehumanisation, leaving practically no room for the growth of profounder, ethical and spiritual consciousness which alone can rightly and wisely guide human volition in taking decisions in the critical times that seem to lie ahead of us. While under the pressure of the technological development, the world is shrinking and we are dreaming of the possibility of a planetary civilisation, we have not yet the required corresponding psychological development which can enable the human consciousness and character to sustain such a planetary civilisation.

On the contrary, there is growing preponderance of those impulses which can thrive only through ignorance, fragmentation, discord and violence. As we study the situation, we feel convinced that it is a vain chimera to believe that the world of today and tomorrow can be safe without a radical change in human consciousness and character. It is true that the wisest leaders of today have declared unambiguously that the future of the human race is dependent exclusively upon a radical transformation of human consciousness, and that one of the most important means of effecting this transformation is an integral and value-oriented education. Unfortunately, this counsel is heard dimly and ignored greatly when we frame our plans of action for education.

It is, therefore, necessary that a voluntary effort is initiated and conferences, seminars and workshops are organised where the theme of integral and value-oriented education and the theme of education for character development are studied in depth. It is only through this method that a wide awakening among people can be generated. Without this awakening, such a difficult thing as education for character development cannot be conceived and implemented.

In the first place, we need to clarify ourselves as to what we mean by education for character development. In simplest terms, character implies well-trained will to be straightforward, fearless and honest coupled with sincerity to act and even to fight nobly and courageously in order to embody in one's own life and in the life of the society all that is true and all that can foster solidarity and unity.

Character may be considered to have four dimensions, dimension of wisdom, dimension of heroic will, dimension of compassion and universal love, and dimension of competence, chiseled skill and untiring labour.

A well-developed character is integrated character; it is able to sharpen in-born capacities and potentialities towards their own highest values. A developed character is a developed personality that harmonises the demands of physical education, vital education, emotional education, of rational education, aesthetic education, ethical and spiritual education.

In our present system of education, all that we have conceived here to be relevant to the development of character is sadly missing. We are too preoccupied with mental development, and even in the field of mental development, we give a preponderant importance to those qualities which are relevant to our present examination system. We are thus not giving so much importance to the development of power of understanding as to the power of memory.

Our education is limited to the imparting of information; we hardly aim at imparting knowledge; and development of wisdom is entirely out of the court. We do not emphasise the learning of *facts*. We do not give importance to the pursuit of truth; we propose only the pursuit of piece-meal assemblage of topics and subjects which are prescribed in our syllabus. It is only recently that some place is being given to physical education and aesthetic education. But the situation is entirely unsatisfactory when we come to the domain of character development. Even our thinking on the subject of values which are central to character development is beset with confusions and doubts. Our first necessity is to explore the basic ideas in regard to values, to determine what they mean and what place they can be given and in what way they can be implemented in our system of education.

Let us dwell a little upon the word "value". This word, as understood in the context of educational philosophy, refers to those desirable ideals and goals which are intrinsic in themselves and which, when achieved or attempted to be achieved, evoke a deep sense of fulfilment to one or many or all parts of what we consider to be the highest elements of our nature. In a sense, it may be urged that the word "value" is basically undefinable, since it denotes a fundamental category and it is itself the highest genus of that category. At the same time, there is a common understanding in regard to truth, beauty and goodness which can be conceived as the supreme values of life.

They are intrinsic in character, and they are ends-in-themselves. Even if there are wide differences as to what is meant by these three terms, there is an agreement that they are most desirable ideals and mere orientation towards them inspires development of those states of our being and becoming in which we can hope to find some kind of ultimate fulfilment.

These three great ideals can guide us in developing all that we have spoken of as character and all that can be considered to be of highest value to integral personality. As a result, in the domain of physical education, we discover the values of health, grace and beauty. In the domain of emotional education, we arrive at the values of harmony and friendliness, of courage and heroism, of endurance and perseverance and of irresistible will to conquer the forces of ignorance, division and injustice. In the sphere of mental education, the values that emerge are those of utmost impartiality, dispassionate search after the Truth, widest possible synthesis, and calm and silence. The values pertaining to the aesthetic development would be those of the vision of Beauty and creative joy of the deepest possible aesthetic experience and expression.

When we come to the field of moral and spiritual values, the situation is rather difficult and complex. Is there, we may ask, any valid distinction between moral and spiritual values? In answer, it may be said that much depends upon what we intend in include in our definition of the word "morality" or in the word "spirituality". In Indian thought, the distinction between morality and spirituality has been clearly made and each one has its specific and distinguishing connotation.

The word "morality" connotes a pursuit of the control and mastery over impulses and desires under the guidance and supervening inspiration of a standard of conduct formulated in consideration of man's station and duties in the society or in consideration of any discovered or prescribed intrinsic law of an ideal. Morality is often conceived as a preparation for spirituality. Spirituality begins when one seeks whatever one conceives to be the ultimate and absolute, for its own sake unconditionally and without any reserve whatsoever. Moreover, while morality is often limited to the domain of duties, spirituality is fundamentally a search of the *knowledge* of the highest and the absolute by direct experience and manifestation of the search in every mode of living, thinking and acting.

Again, both the moral and the spiritual are to be distinguished from what is called "religious" when we speak of religious education. Religion, which can be called *sampradaya* has the following distinguishing features:

— A specific religious belief or creed or doctrine about the nature of Reality, scripture and traditional founder, prophet or incarnation;

— Every specific religion has, as its essential ingredient, certain prescribed acts, rituals and ceremonies;

— A religious authority to which religious matters are referred and the decision of which is final.

Both moral and spiritual values can be practised irrespective of whether one believes in one religion or another or whether one believes in no religion. Both morality and spirituality can be independent of rituals and ceremonies and of any acts specifically prescribed by any particular religion. And both of them are independent of any authority except that of one's own free judgement and direct spiritual experience.

It is also useful to distinguish religion from what in India is called "dharma". Dharma is not any religious creed or dogma and system of rituals but a deeper law of the harmonious and interdependent growth of the deepest aspirations of the collectivity and of the individuals that constitute the collectivity. Dharma can be regarded as an ordered system of moral and spiritual values.

Values that we seek in the moral and spiritual domain are those of sincerity, faithfulness, obedience to whatever one conceives to be the highest, gratitude, selflessness, freedom from egoism, equality in joy and suffering, in honour and dishonour, in success and failure, pursuit of the deepest and the highest, and of the absolute and the ultimate, and progressive expression of this pursuit in thought, feeling and action.

It must be observed that the pursuit of these values is not intrinsically related to any particular religion. These values are intrinsic and ends in themselves, irrespective of whether one holds any particular doctrine of ethics, religion or spirituality. Whether one belongs to one religion or the other, or to no religion, one can pursue these values devotedly and zealously.

Having clarified some of the important elements of education for character development, it is necessary to underline that this education should not be conceived as a training in certain Do's and Don'ts. It may be mentioned that Do's and Don'ts refer to outer actions; and outer actions derive their value only in relation to the inner motive and the inner consciousness from which they emerge. The given right state of consciousness may express itself in different forms of action, and each of these actions would be right, since behind each one of them there is a living vibration of the right state of consciousness. On the other hand, there are several actions which may apparently seem good and right in their outer forms, and yet if they are not spontaneous expressions of the right motive, they cease to have any value from the point of view of character.

It is also to be underlined that education for character development cannot be confined to a specific period in the total framework of a timetable. All occasions of daily life should be utilised to bring the student nearer to the realisation of the ideals of character development. There are occasions when children express wild impulses and passions, and often they are in revolt.

Children have their own daily battles of loyalties and friendships, and there are moments of desperate depression and of violent enthusiasm. There are occasions when children can be vexed, become sulky and go on strike. All these occasions are occasions for education for character development. With patience and perseverance, the teacher can utilise all these occasions to show the truth and light and to awaken among the children the right sense and the right sense of true progress.

It is also to be underlined that in the process of education for character development, character of the teacher is of supreme importance. We are thus required to demand from the teachers a very exacting role. For the fulfilment of this role, teachers themselves must feel inspired to learn the lessons of self-control and to foster harmonious blending of wisdom, will, courage, compassion, harmony, and competences of various kinds that are directly relevant to the tasks of teaching learning process. The teacher should be able to involve his or her total being in the teaching-learning process.

The question here is not merely to deal with subjects and books but also with faculties and capacities, and particularly, with the powers of will and concentration that are indispensable in developing character. The teacher will need to have not only a high degree of proficiency in his or her own subject of discipline but he or she will also need to arrive, as rapidly as possible, at a considerable maturity of the growth of personality, and he or she will need to look upon the work of teaching as a part of the discipline required for the development of his or her own personality and character. Only a teacher of high character can generate students of high character.

Methods of Education for Character Development

At the outset, we need to examine the view that values

cannot be taught and, therefore, character development cannot be a subject matter for teaching. It is argued that there is a valid distinction between pursuit of knowledge and pursuit of character development and that while knowledge can be taught, character development falls outside the purview of the teaching process. But when we examine this view more closely, we find that what is meant is that the methods which are valid and appropriate in the field of learning in regard to knowledge are not applicable to the field of learning in the field of values which are central in the process of development of character.

We may readily accept this contention, and we may insist on the necessity of recognising the fact that corresponding to each domain of learning there are valid and appropriate methods and that the effectivity of learning will depend upon an ever-vigilant discovery of more and more appropriate methods in each domain of learning. It is clear, for example, that while philosophy can be learned and be taught by a process of discussion, swimming cannot be learned and taught by discussion. In order to learn to swim, one has to plunge and swim. Similarly, the methods of learning music or painting have to be quite different from those by which we learn mathematics or physics.

And, indeed, when we come to the realm of character and values, we must recognise the necessity of a greater scruple in prescribing the methods which can be considered to be distinctively appropriate to this field.

One speciality of the domain of character is that it is centrally related to volition and affection rather than to cognition. According to some, education for character development should be exclusively or more or less exclusively limited to certain prescribed acts of volition and that the education for character development should be judged by what a learner *does* rather than what he *knows*. This view is, however, too simplistic and exclusive and we should avoid the rigidity that arises from this kind of gross exclusivism.

There is also an opposite view according to which learning is primarily a cognitive process and, therefore, all the learning processes connected with character development should largely or preponderantly be limited to those methods which are appropriate to cognition. This view, too, is a gross exclusivism which should be avoided. A synthesis of these two views would result in the recommendation that in the processes of education for character development, methods appropriate to volition and affection should be more preponderant but appropriate methods to cognition also should have a legitimate and even an indispensable place. This is reinforced by the fact that the striving towards values stirs up the totality of the being, and cognition no less than volition and affection is or can be stimulated to its highest maximum degrees, provided that the process of learning involved in character development is allowed its natural fullness.

In any sound process of teaching and learning, three instruments which are available to the teacher are: instruction, example and influence. However, in our present system of education, instruction plays an overwhelmingly important role and often when we think of teaching we think only of instruction. It is this illegitimate identification of all teaching with instruction that causes much confusion and avoidable controversies. If we examine the matter carefully, we shall find that in an ideal system of teaching, instruction should play a much less important role than example and influence of the teacher. It is true that in the domain of learning where cognitive activities play a more important part, instruction through lecture and discussion may have, under certain circumstances, a larger role,. But in this domain of learning, where volition and affective activities play a larger part, instruction through methods other than lectures and discussions should play a larger role.

Unfortunately, our present system of education, being what it is, there is such rigidity that example and influence can play very limited effective role. In the present rigid and mechanical structure, the centre of attention is not the child but the book, the teacher, syllabus and the examination. The methods which are most conducive to the development of the character of the child such as the methods of self-learning, exercise of free will, individualised pace of progress, etc., do not have even an elbow room. Indeed, if this is the system of education and if we are to remain content with this system of education, most important elements of learning will for ever remain outside the system, and we cannot confidently recommend any effective system of learning, much less any effective programme of character development.

We must, therefore, envisage that sooner rather than later, our system of education will change in the right direction and increasing number of educationists and teachers must come forward to break the rigidities of our educational system. At the same time, we should also institute the right type of training for teachers so that teachers are oriented towards education for character development.

The change that we should envisage must also propose a radical transformation of our present system of examination. Apart from a number of undesirable aspects of our examination system, the one which is particularly conducive to what may be called "anti-value" is the tendency which promotes the idea that passing of examinations and earning of degree is the aim of education. Radical measures should be adopted to combat this idea and to introduce such changes in our examination system whereby the educational process can remain unalterably fixed on the right aims of education, which must place development of character in centrality. A radical change in the examination system is a necessary condition of any meaningful education for character development.

It is sometimes argued that values can best be taught through the instrumentality of a number of subjects rather than through any specific or special subject, whether we may call it by the name of "moral education" or ethics" or "value-education". There is no doubt a great force behind this contention and we may readily agree that we must have a well-conceived programme of studies of various subjects which would naturally provide, both in their content and thrust, the requisite materials for character development.

The question, however, is whether our current programmes of studies have been or are being so carefully devised so as to emphasis those aspects which can rightly provide to teachers and students the required opportunities, conditions and materials for character development. A massive work remains to be done in this connection.

At the same time, it may be suggested that even if our programmes of studies of various subjects are revised, there will still remain the specific areas of values which should receive a special, although not exclusive, attention and treatment. In other words, there seems to be a good ground to recommend that there should be, in the totality of educational programmes, a *core* programme of value-education and character development.

This core programme should, however, be so carefully devised that various threads of this progrmme are woven into the complex totality of all the other programmes of studies. The point to be underlined is that the central theme of education for character development would not form a mere appendage of all other subjects but would stand out as the overarching and the supervening subject of basic importance.

It is sometimes suggested that education for character development or value-oriented education is relevant only to the primary and secondary stages, but not beyond. For, it is argued, children by the time they complete secondary education would have already formed their basic attitudes, their traits of personality and their character, and nothing more needs to be done specially in that direction at the higher levels of education. But this argument misses the point that the important element in the development of character is the development of free-will and of the learner's free and rational acceptance of the value system and directions of the growth of character and personality. And this development can rightly be done only at the higher levels of education, when the learner has developed a will of his own to some extent and when he has basic intellectual and moral and aesthetic sensibilities enabling him to examine the basic values and aims of life.

The fundamental aims of higher education include the pursuit of clarity of thought, search for perfection, irresistible will to realise "*summum bonum*" and higher humanistic, scientific and professional skills. These are also essential requisites of integral development of personality and character. It is this that necessitates us to recommend that education for character development should also form a central focus of higher education.

The secret of education for character development is the way in which the teacher can inspire and kindle the quest among the students by means of one's own example of character and mastery of knowledge that is relevant to the over-arching importance of character both in the individual life and in the collective life. It is only by embodying values within oneself that the teacher can really radiate values to students.

While laying a great emphasis on the role of the teacher in respect of education for character development, it must be emphasised that education is a sub-system of society, and, therefore, the role of the society in stimulating and supporting aims of character development must be underlined. In this connection, two social actions may be suggested. Firstly, society must place the child in the centre of its attention and declare the sovereignty of the child. It must resolve to bestow upon the child the supreme care that it needs. It will organise all activities and also special activities in such a way that they become vehicles of character development of the child. And, secondly, just as the child always looks to the future, the society, too, will constantly strive to build the paths of the future. Just as child will grow increasingly into the vigorous and dynamic youth, the society also must continue to learn and to mature so as to manifest unfailing youthfulness. The society should recommend to all members to continue to learn and to grow so as to actualise a learning society.

The task of the teacher who aims at the character development of the child is to put the child upon the right road to its own perfection and to encourage it to follow that road, watching, suggesting, helping, but not imposing or interfering. The best method of suggestion is by personal example, daily conversation and books read from day-to-day. These books should contain, for the younger students, the lofty examples of the past, given not as moral lessons but as things of supreme human interest, and for the older students, great thoughts of great souls, passages of literature, which set fire to the highest emotions and prompt the highest ideals and aspirations, records of history and biographies which exemplify the living of those great thoughts, noble emotions and inspiring ideals.

Opportunities should be given to the students by embodying in actions the deeper and nobler impulses which rise within them.

An informal but profound study of the following questions would prove to be of immense value:

— What is action? How does it operate normally? Can action be controlled and guided? How can one achieve the maximum effectivity and larger scope of action?

— To whom should I belong? What is the meaning of allegiance? What is the highest to which my highest allegiance should be given?

— What is the purpose of the human body? What are the means by which the perfection of the body can be achieved?

— What are the highest means of knowledge? Is there something which being known, everything can be known?

— What is the nature of the mind? How does it operate in (a) scientific thinking, (b) mathematical thinking, and (c) philosophical thinking? It is possible to attain to a total state of concentration and even to arrive at total silence?

— How can we arrive at an artistic and creative experience? What is the essence of music? What is the essence of art? What is the essence of literature?

— What is the indispensable utility of technology in the human life and its perfection?

— What is the meaning of story? Is history an interesting and meaningful story? Is there an aim in history? What are lessons of history?

— What am I? And what is my own specific role in the world? How can I train myself to fulfil this role?

One can formulate many more questions but care should be taken to see that these questions and topics do not get compressed within a rigid framework of a formal study and examination. These are all living questions and the only thing that can be done is to see that they arise spontaneously during the educational process, and the courses of study regarding them develop in an evolutionary way, developing with inner growth of the students. It is best when these questions arise in the context of the living experience of the students.

The handling of these questions and topics should be informal and the following methods can be suggested:

— Each student should be suggested to choose from a list of questions, and he should be free to choose any one of them in accordance with his needs of a deep inquiry;

— students should study these questions individually with a possibility of consultation with their teachers when needed;

— to enable individual study, the teachers should suggest relevant materials or books, or else he should prepare special worksheets;

— informal talks on these questions can be arranged, but they should not take the form of any moral or religious preaching; the temper of these studies should be scientific, interesting and profound;

— there should be a room of Silence in every school and college, and students should be free to go to that room, whenever they wish to have an inner reflection, meditation or quiet study;

— seminars on the relevant questions and topics should be held periodically in the school and colleges and the students and teachers should be encouraged to participate in them;

— debates, too, can be organised relating to these questions and topics, but an attempt should be made at the end of every debate to synthesize various points of view; an idea must develop that behind every point of view there is some truth, and we should grow into a comprehensive vision in which all truths can be reconciled and synthesized, and in which all conflicting views can be transcended;

— artistic books and sculptural pieces relating to these questions and topics should be displayed prominently not only in schools and colleges, but everywhere in towns, villages, etc.;

— other media of communication should also be widely used for this purpose. In particular, society should produce films relating to these subjects and they should be made available to students and teachers;

— informality in instruction, joy in learning, utter dedication and strictness in training, and wide comprehension in student-teacher relationship – these will, in brief, govern the methods of learning.

There are aspects of the mental, vital and physical education which contribute to the development of character. The methods in regard to these that have emerged through various experimentations can be suggested as follows:

— In its natural state, the human mind is always limited in its vision, narrow in its understanding, rigid in its conceptions and a special effort is need to enlarge it, make it supple and deep. Hence, it is very necessary to develop in the child the inclination and capacity to consider everything from as many points of view as possible. There is an exercise in this connection which gives greater suppleness and elevation to thought. It is as follows. A clearly formulated thesis is set; against it is opposed the anti-thesis, formulated with the same precision. Then by careful reflection the problem must be widened or transcended so that a synthesis is found which unites the two contraries in a larger, higher and more comprehensive idea.

— Another exercise is to control the mind from judging things and people. For true knowledge belongs to a region much higher than that of the human mind, even beyond that of pure ideas. The mind has got to be made silent and attentive in order to receive knowledge from above and manifest it.

— Still another exercise: whenever there is a disagreement on any matter, as a decision, as a decision to take, or an action to accomplish, one must not stick to one's own conception or point of view. On the contrary, one must try to understand the other person's point of view, put oneself in his place and, instead of quarrelling or even fighting, find out a solution which can reasonably satisfy both parties; there is always one for people of good will.

— A wide, subtle, rich, complex, attentive and quiet and silent mind is an asset not only for the discovery of the deeper ethical, aesthetic, psychic and spiritual realities, but also for manifesting their truths and powers.

— The vital being in us is the seat of impulses and desires, of enthusiasm and violence, of dynamic energy and desperate depression, of passions and revolt. The vital is a good worker, but most often it seeks its own satisfaction. If that is refused totally or even partially, it gets vexed, sulky and goes on strike.

- An exercise at these moments is to remain quiet and refuse to act. For it is important to realise that at such times one does stupid things and in a few minutes can destroy or spoil what one has gained in months of regular effort, losing thus all the progress made.
- Another exercise is to deal with the vital as one deals with a child in revolt, with patience perseverance showing it the truth and light, endeavoring to convince it and awaken in it the goodwill which for a moment was veiled.
- A wide, strong, clam but dynamic vital capable of right emotion, right decision, and right execution by force and energy, is an invaluable aid to the psychic and spiritual realisation.
- The body by its nature is a docile and faithful instrument. But it is very often misused by the mind with its dogmas, its rigid and arbitrary principles, and by the vital with its passions, its excesses and dissipations. It is these which are the cause of bodily fatigue, exhaustion and disease. The body must therefore be free from the tyranny of the mind and of the vital; and this can be done by training the body to feel and sense the psychic presence within and to learn to obey its governance. The emphasis on the development of strength, suppleness, calm, quiet, poise, grace and beauty in physical education, whether done by *Yogic Asanas* or by other methods of physical culture, such as games and sports, or Japanese Judo and similar exercise will ensure the contact of the body with the psychic centre and the body will learn to put forth at every minute the effort that is demanded of it; for it will have learnt to find rest in action, to replace through contact with universal forces the energies it spends consciously and usefully. Bu this sound and balanced life, a new

> harmony will manifest in the body, reflecting the harmony of the regions which will give it the perfect proportions and the ideal beauty of form. It will then be in a constant process of transformation, and it will be possible for it to escape the necessity of disintegration and destruction.

The role that physical education can play in the development of character has not been sufficiently understood. In our country, physical education has been neglected almost completely and this neglect is one of the causes of the low morale of the people. It is, therefore, necessary to bring forth the value of physical education not only in regard to the fitness of the body but also for the great contribution it makes for the intellectual, moral and spiritual development of character and personality.

It has been found necessary by recent research in yogic education that students should develop a high sense of physical culture and a bodily need of daily physical exercise. Our programme in schools and colleges should be so organised that everyday a student is able to devote at least one hour for physical education, either in the form of *Yogic Asanas* and allied exercise or in the form of gymnastics, athletics, aquatics or games.

There are many sports which help to form and necessitate the qualities of courage, hardihood, energetic action and initiative for skill, steadiness of will or rapid decision and action, the perception of what is to be done in an emergency and dexterity in doing it. Another invaluable result of these activities is the growth of the sporting spirit. That includes good humour and tolerance and consideration for all, a right attitude and friendliness to competitors and rivals, self-control and scrupulous observance of the laws of the games, fair play and avoidance of the use of foul means, an equal acceptance of victory or defeat without bad humour, resentment or ill-will towards successful competitors, loyal acceptance of the decisions of the appointed judge, umpire or referee. More important still is the custom of discipline, obedience, order, habit of team work, which certain games necessitate.

In the words of Sri Aurobindo :

> "If they (the above qualities) could be made more common not only in the life of the individual but in the national life and in the international where at the present day the opposite tendencies have become too rampant, existence in this troubled world of ours would be smoother and might open to a greater chance of concord and amity of which it stands very much in need...The nation which possesses them in the highest degree is likely to be strongest for victory, success and greatness, but also for the contribution it can make towards the bringing about of unity and more harmonious world order towards which we look as our hope for humanity's future."

At higher levels of education, it may be suggested that a critical study of values is itself an essential part of value-education. Exploration of all that mankind has thought on this subject should suitably be presented to the students, so that they have before them a wide spectrum of ideas which they can explore and experiment with. Topics such as man in the universe, aim of human life, concept of progress, definition of values, and ideals of liberty, equality and fraternity could be recommended as a necessary part of a special programme of character development.

Since values are those desirable ideals and goals which are intrinsic in themselves, and which, when achieved, or attempted to be achieved, have a deep sense of fulfilment of one or many or all parts and faculties of personality, it is necessary that the programme of character development should include a study of faculties and capacities that constitute our personality and the correlation of each faculty with its corresponding values.

Science and values should also be an important part of character development. Pursuit of the value of truth through science and self-knowledge as also the correlation of science and values with the theme of progress and welfare of human mind should be an important part of the progrmme.

A study of ethical thought as also religious and spiritual thought should also be a part of the programme of exploration. These will include the study of good and evil, comparative study of religions, and the psychology of yogic sciences.

Since art is also a great gate to the perception and practice of the value of Beauty, this also should form a part of the proposed programme.

Value of harmony of the human being with nature and ecological balance should also find an appropriate place in the proposed programme.

A study of the value of physical education and of the qualities that make an ideal sports-person should also be treated as an integral part of education for character development.

To fulfil the highest aims of education for character development, the aim that should be put forward before students of higher education is to learn to learn and to learn throughout life so as to arrive in due course a solid mass of knowledge that can illumine, by an incessant downpour of its sheer lustre, the universal skies and the hidden and distant secrets of Matter, a most potent drive of energy and heroic action, and an irresistible bursting forth of love, joy and marvellous forms of beauty. Presentation of this ideal in an effective manner would infuse a new spirit and stimulate education for character development.

Contents of Education and Character Development

Methods and contents of education are interrelated; this is particularly true in respect of education for character development, where methods themselves are in significant measure contents. This is the reason why the treatment of these two subjects tends to have some kind of overlapping. In a sense, the teacher in respect of education for character development has no method and yet every method. Similarly, he has no specific content and yet every content. A simple statement like the one that was given to Shvetaketu by his father, "Thou art That," can become sufficient for the entirety of the contents, and mere meditation would suffice as entirety of method. But this would not suffice in each and every case or when we have to deal with a large number of students, where each individual will need to have a special programme appropriate to his or her needs of growth and his or her special approach and method of growth. It is for this reason that we need to formulate methods and contents in a somewhat general way which can guide the teachers in dealing with such a difficult and subtle subject as education for character development.

It must have been observed that while expounding the methods, we have restrained ourselves to generalities, since what the teacher has to do in specific situations or in specific stages of each of his students has to be determined by him, and no specific prescriptions can be made in advance. In the same way, if we are to present a programme or a curriculum in regard to the contents, it can only be in the form of a very general guideline, and it has to be implemented by the teacher not as a fixed framework of a rigid syllabus, but as flexible and experimental set of ideas and suggestions. The teacher has to feel free to modify, enrich or alter it in an experimental manner while dealing with his students in specific situations or in specific stages of development.

An exploratory draft programme which is being presented here should be looked up in this light.

When we study the concept of character development in all its aspects, one central thing that emerges is that the entire processor character development is ultimately reduced to the process of self-knowledge and the process of self-control. In our undeveloped condition, we are a complex of impulses and passions, of rudimentary faculties and capacities and of inarticulate ideas and aspirations. All these need to be developed by three basic processes: introspective observation, careful processes of control, and growing awareness of oneself and of the world and their interrelationship by means of refinement of faculties and capacities. The more we observe ourselves and the more we control our impulses and passions in the right manner, the more we discover what we are truly in our deepest depths and highest heights and how we can deal with the world in a manner by which we can act rightly and contribute to the increasing progress and unification of the society and the world. This entire process can be covered under the general theme of character development, and this theme can best be described under the general title: "To know oneself and to control oneself".

There are three important elements which have magnetic power to lift students from lower to higher levels of character. These are: illumination, love, and heroism. Illumination is basically the experience of clarity in respect of understanding of inner states of consciousness, of widening horizons of environment, and of value of relationships and internal complexities of psychological and physical life. At a lower level, this clarity is conceptual, but as we ascend higher and higher, it assumes the nature of intuitive and inspirational enlightenment. Love is that indefinable but powerful force of delight that ultimately brings about harmony in all relations. As Shelley pointed out, "This is the bond and the sanction which connects not only men with men but everything which exists."

Transcending selfishness and self-centredness, love opens its portal to the inner cave of our hearts and makes us surrender to the supreme glory that is universal and divine. Heroism is spontaneous galloping of power that rides on crest of self-giving which cares only for establishment of justice and upholding of all that is noble and true. These three, in their combination provide irresistible leverage for rising into a transforming process. They render the tasks of self-control into the tasks of transmutation. Not suppression but rejection, purification and sublimation of the lower impulses and drives is the real secret of self-control.

One of the important instruments by which these three elements can be made operative in the educational process is that of good stories. A programme of character development must provide for a large number of stories that illustrate the themes of illumination, love and heroism. But care should be taken to ensure that these stories should have been written in a language that is chaste and beautiful. They can be selected from the world literature but made available to the children in the language which they all understand and appreciate. They should be full of human interest, and they should be able to create an atmosphere that is clean and uplifting.

Along with stories, selections from poems and plays should also be a part of the programme. Inspiring passages and interesting essays also should be utilised.

Exhibitions play a great role in creating collective atmosphere and also in opening vaster vision and imagination.

The programme should also include exercises of contemplation, purification and of aesthetic experience.

Nobility of character is greatly sustained by the mind which is both wide and profound and which aspires to reach higher levels of knowledge. A great effort needs to be made, therefore, to ensure that learning material should have a vast canvas where the East and the West can meet and where subtlety are complexity of life are portrayed in a stimulating manner. Subjects and topics must be presented which develop sense of wonder.

There are a number of topics which are directly related to self-knowledge; there are others which aim at giving a synoptic view of the world; there are topics which are concerned with themes of mutuality, harmony and true brotherhood. All these topics should suitably be presented in a well-graded manner.

Linguistic capacities are a great aid to the development of character. The greater the mastery over the language, the greater is the mastery over thought; and the greater the mastery over thought, the greater is the power of controlling the lower by the higher. The programme should, therefore, provide exercises that aim at chiseling the capacities of linguistic expression, both oral and written. The exercise in this connection should also include those of recitation, singing, and dramatics.

Works of labour and community service with an inner sense of dedication should be underlined. The right attitude towards work should also be cultivated; it must be remembered that one must work, not to come first but to do one's very best, that one must work to achieve perfection and one must be neither in a great hurry nor lazy and sluggish.

One of the important aspects of the programme should be related to bridge the gap between the realms of science and the realm of values. The perception of the unity of the world is a necessary basis for durable striving for harmony and brotherhood. There are a number of topics that could be suggested which would show the unity of Master, Life, and Mind; and there are various other topics which could show the possibilities of developing mind to manifest higher powers that would, in due course, promote higher levels of harmony. These topics should be presented in a graded manner so that one begins to perceive how the entire world-process is one and how a true harmony between oneself and humanity can be established.

At higher levels in secondary or higher secondary courses, introductory topics which would provide reflections on religion, science, philosophy and Yoga should form an important part of studies. As these subjects are full of complexities and controversies, great care should be taken to prepare learning materials that would encourage impartiality and comparative studies. Instead of providing dogmatic answers, we need to develop the sense of exploration in the growing minds of students.

In the end, it may be emphasised that since character development is related predominantly to will, and since will is well developed when we provide freedom of choice, special emphasis should be laid on creating environment where students can enjoy freedom. Freedom necessarily raises questions regarding discipline. Ideally, discipline should be a resultant of freedom, and all discipline should be self-discipline. One of the most difficult problems in character development is as to how to inspire students to impose on themselves a programme of self-discipline. The success of the programme of education for character development will depend upon how far the contents and methods of education can harmonise the demands of freedom and discipline. It is worth remembering the famous view of Socrates, that is, only when we are utterly free that we cannot but choose the good and the right.

The programme that is presented here aims at providing a flexible framework of the study and practice of those elements which would directly or indirectly promote the basic elements of character development. It is an attempt to correlate main aspects of what Swami Vivekananda spoke in regard to man-making education with the varieties of subjects that are normally pursued in the primary, secondary and higher secondary courses in Indian schools.

This programme underlines those elements of education which seem to be indispensable for every one to grow up as a well-developed human being, irrespective of what specialties are chosen for specialisation. Everyone needs to know the mystery and excellence of the human body, since the body is the material base of the pursuit of whatever ideals one chooses to embody in one's individual and social life. Everyone needs to understand one's own impulses, desires, emotions and will power in order to determine how to control and master them and even transform them so that one grows into a personality guided by wisdom and inspired by the sense of harmony and heroic courage. Everyone needs to know how mind functions and how rationality, morality, and aesthetic refinement grow into higher and deeper reaches of psychic and spiritual being.

Everyone needs to practise attitude and powers of concentration and harmonisation of inner and outer life. Everyone needs to learn how to learn and how to continue to learn throughout life. Everyone needs to be a good pupil and a good teacher and everyone needs to develop the capacity to choose the right aim of life and to pursue that aim with determination and perseverance. Finally, everyone needs to have basic grounding to be able to ask: What is the mystery of this world and one's own place in it so as to be able to play one's role effectively?

These and allied subjects need to be woven together in a graded manner so that the teacher can aid the student in a very flexible manner in the process of growth of character. As stated above, the key-words of the growth are "to know oneself" and "to control oneself". It is to be underlined that both these are difficult, but to render them into processes of supreme interest and unfailing enthusiasm is a task that can be fulfilled only if we chalk out a programme that is psychologically sound and practically workable. Much will depend upon the teacher's skills and powers of inspiration and guidance. And much will also depend upon the quality of the teaching-learning material that will be provided by the educators.

With these introductory remarks, a draft programme is presented. This programme is tentative, and this presentation is really in the form of invitation to the participants to study it and to suggest ways and means by which it can be improved and implemented. It will be seen that this programme will require the production of relevant teaching-learning material. It will also demand from teachers new attitudes and new initiatives and dedication. This may also imply a new programme of training of teachers. A good deal of cooperation has to be sought from parents and all those who are connected with the development of children. It may also be necessary to initiate courses of training of parents and others. This will, again, demand the task of preparing the relevant teaching-learning material.

One of the purposes of this presentation is to involve the participants in a long-term exercise through which the required teaching-learning material can be produced, experimented upon and brought to some kind of perfection.

8

ICTs and Teacher Education

In view of the profound and multi-dimensional impact of new ICT on education and on society, this discussion goes beyond its simple use for teaching-learning purposes. It requires a fundamental rethinking on the three-way interaction between education, technology and development. It also necessitates a general consideration of how knowledge can be made accessible in an information society, through formal education and through non-formal as well as informal systems.

In emerging knowledge-based economies and information-intensive societies, technology now increasingly serves both education and development goals. 'Knowledge and information' are the new forms of wealth and are the driving force for development. The main challenge is how to ensure equal access of all to the means of acquiring necessary skills in a changed environment, and how to use technology to facilitate the education and training of the population for development purposes.

The strong three-way link binding development, education and technology constitutes a deep and systemic argument that ties investment not only with progress in education, but (more importantly) also with the development process itself. It represents the key strand in a reciprocal link through which development, education and technology can become mutually reinforcing within a dynamic framework for progress. It also represents what is increasingly seen as a fundamental human right for every citizen to have access in a global era. This, in a sense, equates education with 'empowerment for development'.

Over the decades, the evolving concept of 'development' has been broadened from increasing production of goods and services to include equitable distribution of wealth, active participation in decision-making, protection of the environment, and preservation of cultural identity. Development refers to growth that is equitable, sustainable and people-centred.

The UNDP Human Development Report in 1990 made the far-reaching statement that people are the wealth of a nation and that human development is a process of broadening people's choices. UNDP-proposed Human Development Indicators have included adult literacy and educational attainment level in terms of combined primary, secondary and tertiary gross enrolment. 'Development of the people' denotes investment in human capabilities through education and the development of skills that aid progress. Development by the people also means giving everyone a chance to participate in the process of growth and development. Development, therefore, has an economic dimension as well as social, environmental, cultural and scientifictechnological aspects.

Education has a fundamental role in empowering people of all ages to assume responsibility for creating a sustainable future. Human development is an important means to technology development. Technological innovation is an expression of human potential.

Education is both a fundamental means to, and an end to, personal and social development. Education provides a significant knowledge base that underpins technological development. Human development and technological advances can be mutually reinforcing, thereby creating 'a virtuous circle'.

In socio-economic terms, education is a tool for poverty alleviation and social inclusion. In cultural terms, education is an instrument for transmission of cultural values from generation to generation and for nurturing creativity in young minds. Education taps the potential of individual learners towards its fullest development. It requires a trained workforce and specialists who can advance new technologies, and it creates new knowledge towards cutting edge technology.

Technology has always been a powerful tool for human development and a major driving force of national growth. In the 21st Century, it is development that will unleash human capacity and create technological enhancement. No development is possible without the help of science and technology. Meanwhile, the direction and pace of technology development are greatly influenced by national development programmes. Human development lies at the heart of policy of all countries and high priority is invariably given to strategies for technological as well as educational development.

The new forms of ICT have had a profound impact on human activities concerned with economic production, work and life just as much as with education and training. In today's information society, new technological development is creating a cultural and educational environment capable of diversifying the sources of knowledge and learning. The new forms of ICT have great potential in contributing to human development in the 21st Century.

Firstly, newly developed ICT provides vital input to almost all human activities and can be used in the most varied locations and for multiple purposes.

Secondly, ICT breaks barriers to human development in at least three ways, which were not possible earlier [3]. ICT facilitates knowledge as it enables universal access to information, which is as central as education is towards enhancing human capabilities. While education develops cognitive skills, information gives content to knowledge. State-of-the-art ICT, especially the Intranet and the World Wide Web, can deliver information to anyone, anytime, anywhere.

New ICT involves innovations in microelectronics, computing (hardware and software), telecommunications and opto-electronics - microprocessors, semiconductors, and fibre optics. These innovations enable the processing and storage of an enormous amount of information and the rapid distribution of information through communication networking. Networks now have wider reach and falling costs due to accelerated development in ICT and galloping globalisation. For example, the amount of information that required a whole month and the entire Internet to send in 1997 could be sent over a single cable in a second in 2001. Besides, the cost of transmitting a trillion bits of information from one sub continent to another has fallen drastically.

Rapid advances in new ICT have brought new possibilities and opportunities for still greater advances in human development. The Internet has grown exponentially, from 16 million users in 1995 to more than 400 million users in 2000 and to an expected 1 billion users in 2005. Connectivity is rising at spectacular rates in Europe, Japan, the USA and in many developing countries.

The new ICT has broken down old barriers of time and space. It has made it possible to generate, store, transmit, retrieve and process information and knowledge at increased speeds and with increased efficiency and flexibility. In short, new ICT has opened up almost unlimited possibilities, for teachers and students in terms of information flow and human communication. But it needs to be pointed out that while the advanced ICT offers unprecedented learning opportunities, it does not offer simple solutions to the complex challenges in education and development.

While it is a fundamental human right of children, youth and adults to basic education of relevance and quality, universal basic education is an unfulfilled dream in many countries of the region. To achieve Education for All (EFA) goals, 'improved teaching and learning' implies quality education for all learners, and not only the 'best education for the best few'. Towards this EFA goal, improved access and equity can be made the precondition or the first principle of quality education. ICT can play a major role in ensuring quality in view of the following aspects:

— ICT improves access and promote equity in education
— ICT improves the quality of teaching and learning
— ICT improves management and efficiency of education

Technologies such as CD-ROM, radio and cable. television, or a mix of technologies, can be combined with the Internet to expand its reach. For example, community radio can be used as a gateway to the Internet for its listeners in remote rural areas. Regional/international cooperation can reduce the cost of access to the Internet. The development of ICT has provided improved tools for learning through a global network and wireless technologies enable developing countries with little telecommunications infrastructure to connect to the network.

Many universities in the Asia-Pacific region have implemented web-based education systems. Mega or open universities such as the Open University in the UK, the Indira Gandhi National Open University in India and the Central Radio & TV University in China have extended their communication capabilities to impart lifelong education and training, especially to those living in rural or remote areas. The Internet is serving a growing number of learners, in varied learning environments, along with a larger number of those using a wide range of communication technologies.

The quality and orientation of education at each level and the link with the demand for skills are critical for mastering technology. Quality primary education develops basic capabilities for human development and enables the young to be more innovative and productive. Quality secondary and higher education are also crucial to technology development. Universities not only deliver but also create knowledge and create national capacity to adapt technology to the country's needs and help manage the risks inherent in technological change.

Countries in the Asia-Pacific region have all developed policies and strategies to link educational goals to those of technology and development. ICT has been most rapidly spreading across educational systems as well as in businesses, commerce and other areas of activity. The number of Internet users in China alone has grown to more than 80 million in early 2004, second only to the USA.

However, there are large disparities in the levels of development. The digital divide is most apparent both among countries within the region and within the countries. Internet users are predominantly the following population groups.

Urban, and peri-urban regions: In China, the 15 least developed provinces, with 600 million people, have only 4 million users, while Shanghai and Beijing, with 27 million people, have 5 million users. Among India's 1.4 million Internet connections, more than 1.3 million are in five States.

JFIT PROGRAMME IN ICT EDUCATION

The UNESCO-implemented programme sponsored by the Japanese Funds-in-Trust (JFIT) is based on the fact that the rapid development of ICT presents development agencies with a unique opportunity to take a major multi-pronged approach to the expansion and reforms of education in the Asia-Pacific region. This would help to achieve the overarching goals of EFA. The UNESCO vision is for a system-wide reform at the macro-level, and for change in teaching and learning processes at the micro-level. It is important to recognize that ICT in itself is not going to radically change education systems for the better or miraculously achieve the goals of EFA. A comprehensive view of what education ideally seeks to achieve is needed for ICT to be utilized to its full potential.

The focus of the programme is on how to use ICT to reduce disparities in both educational access and quality of education. Its special concern for gender issues in use of ICT in education will help promote the call of the EFA Framework for gender equality in education by the year 2015. UNESCO envisions that the ICT programme will result in an educational environment involving enriched curricula, resources sharing, quality multimedia material, and a cadre of teachers who are competent in facilitating better learning through ICT.

The most successful ICT-in-education policy would mean nothing without the support of the teachers. Teachers are central to education, and at the core of this proposed programme. The aim of teachers would be to integrate ICT with traditional pedagogy to transform and facilitate learning.

The JFIT project on 'Training and Professional Development of Teachers and Other Facilitators for Effective Use of ICT for Improving Teaching and Learning' focuses primarily on developing the skills of teachers towards integrating ICT into the curriculum. There is an overall project for the region and three other projects that pinpoint the training needs in specified disadvantaged regions.

In accordance with the priorities identified by JFIT, the Bangkok-based UNESCO Asia and Pacific Regional Bureau for Education, UNESCO Member States, the project is aimed at building national capacity in effective use of ICT in education. The Government of Japan has been one of the main sources of funding for the ICT in Education project.

Development Objectives

The Asia-Pacific Programme of Educational Innovation for Development (APEID), which is coordinated by UNESCO, aims at building the capacity of teachers and other facilitators in integrating ICT as a tool in the teaching-learning process. It also aims at tapping the potential of new ICT for improving educational quality through the professional development of teachers, and for reducing disparities within the region as well as within individual countries in terms of learning achievement.

Immediate Objectives

The immediate objectives are as follows:

1. To improve the capability of teachers/facilitators, through both pre-service education and in-service training, in integrating ICT as a pedagogical tool.
2. To identify, create and disseminate country/location-specific ICT pedagogies and models of teachers' use of ICT for different learning environments for which:
   — ICT models for various learning environments are to be created.
   — Country-specific, case-based pedagogies for active learning with ICT are to be developed and pilot tested.
   — Changes in teaching and learning to be assessed, results and lessons learned are to be shared.
3. To develop and put into operation a regional online teacher resource base and an offline network for sharing teacher-developed education courseware. At the same time, to encourage innovative practices in the effective use of ICT as a teaching tool and as an educational resource. These activities will be undertaken in cooperation with different countries of the region and with UNESCO's Regional Clearinghouse on ICT in Education for Asia and the Pacific.

These can be achieved by:

— developing a regional guideline on technology-pedagogy integration and competencybased standards of ICT infusion by teachers

— creating prototype course materials for pre-service teacher education and training modules for in-service teacher training

— designing templates of ICT-integrated e-lesson plans and evaluation tools for teachers to assess their students' learning using ICT

- training teacher educators through 'training of trainers' workshops at regional/ sub-regional and at national/local levels, who will, in turn, train much larger numbers of teachers
- developing and pilot testing country-specific models and pedagogies in ICT integration by teachers, institutional heads and education managers
- cultivating an online teacher resource base to support teachers and institutional heads in integrating ICT in classroom teaching and school-based management
- creating an offline network of teacher training centres to share innovative practices sharing products outside the pilot countries to gather feedback, to identify and reward the most innovative e-lesson plans and ICT integration pedagogies, and for the inclusion of international resources The countries included in this project are Afghanistan, People's Republic of China, Fiji, India, Indonesia, Kazakhstan, Laos PDR, Malaysia, Mongolia, Philippines, Thailand and Vietnam.

ICT Integration

There are various emerging topics in pedagogy-technology integration that are becoming more and more important in the context of innovative teaching and learning practices. The rapid advances of ICT technology principally facilitated these changes.

E-learning

The link between distance lèarning and telecommunications is becoming even stronger, yielding new solutions to old problems, innovative educational resources and new teaching/learning practices. One of the most innovative and promising outcomes of this relationship is e-learning and online education, notably a process whereby teachers and students are linked up in an electronic media/computer network.

The concept of e-learning and how it relates to effective use of ICT is critically important for teacher education, because it places the focus firmly where it should be - jointly on pedagogy and the new ICT. The term e-learning, or learning via electronic media, nicely combines this twin concept: first, the changing focus of pedagogy to learning and, second, the new technologies stretching beyond the walls of the traditional classroom. In other words, e-learning for teacher development is learning about, with, and through all electronic media (i.e., ICT) across the curriculum to support student learning. ICT is the means, and e-learning and the effective integration of pedagogy and ICT constitute the goal. There are a number of benefits to e-learning. These include any time learning, anywhere learning, asynchronous interaction and group collaboration.

Blogs

Blogs or classroom web logs are becoming increasingly popular with teachers and teacher education. Many experts predict that blogs will eventually become more successful teaching tools than web sites. A blog is a web page made up of usually short, frequently updated posts that are arranged chronologically-like a "what's new" page of a journal. The contents and the purposes of blogs vary greatly, from links and commentary about other web sites to news about a company/person/idea, photos, poetry, mini-essays, project updates, even fictions. A crucial blog mission is to link to other web sites, or, sometimes even other blogs.

Many blogs are personal. Others are collaborative efforts based on a specific topic or an area of mutual interest. The use of blogs in instructional settings is limited only by one's imagination. There are many ways teachers can use blogs, some of them include content-related blog, networking and personal knowledge sharing, instructional tips for learners, course announcements and readings, annotated links etc., most importantly for the purpose of knowledge management. Learners can also take part in blogs by reflective writing, assignment submission, collaborative work, e-portfolios and sharing course-related resources.

For teachers, blogs are attractive because it needs little efforts to maintain, unlike more elaborate classroom web sites. Teachers can build a blog or start a new topic in an existing blog by simply typing text into a box and clicking a button. Such ease of use is the primary reason to predict that blogs are more successful teaching tools than web sites.

Pedagogical Content Knowledge

Pedagogy cannot exist in isolation to contents. In fact, there is a new beginning to appreciate that the two intertwined into what is described as Pedagogical Content Knowledge (PCK), and is an essential tenet in the current thinking about teacher education. The term content refers to far more than factual information. It encompasses all aspects of a subject: concept, principles, relationships, methods of inquiry and outstanding issues.

According to the National Science Teachers Association (NSTA), meaning of content to a science teacher is: (a) concepts and principles understood through science; (b) concepts and relationships unifying science domains; (c) processes of investigation in a science discipline; and (d) applications of mathematics in science research. Similarly, the pedagogy component includes actions and strategies of teaching, organization of classroom experiences, providing for diverse learner needs, evaluation and implementation based on learner's prior notions, and transformation of ideas into understandable episodes.

The NSTA Standards accurately identify major problems with respect to pedagogy and contents. It states:

> [There is] "...a poor match between learner needs and teaching methodology", ..."in many traditionally taught courses the emphasis is on learning large amounts of information at a rapid pace", ...and ..... "division of knowledge, for convenience into disciplines, fields and sub fields"..... that ....."may contain the development of linkages among concepts across fields". This is similar to what Shulman had observed, "the key to distinguishing the knowledge base of teaching lies at the intersection of content and pedagogy".

The blend of content and pedagogical knowledge includes understanding why some learners experience difficulties when learning a particular concept, while others find it easy to assimilate knowledge about useful ways to conceptualize and represent a chosen concept. The basic principles of PCK is to make teaching and learning: (a) engaging and motivating; (b) interactive; (c) contextual; (d) reducing cognitive load; (e) scaffolding; and (f) collaborative.

With ICT, there are better ways and opportunities to make above principles more realistic learning experiences. ICT encourages interactions, development of collaborative culture, utilization of active learning and introduction of feedback in proper context. ICT can bring abstract concept to life by bringing into the teaching and learning the real world experiences through simulating, modelling, capturing and analyzing real event.

All instructional designers agree on the need for effective planning of the design and development process. The success of the process largely depends on the preparation of a document, often called a lesson plan with essential elements such as clear indications of what will be done, how it will be done, when it will be done and, more importantly, how technology is going to be used. It has been observed that several prominent theories such as constructivism, sociocultural concept, situated cognition, multiple intelligences, distributed cognition, problem-based learning etc., play an important role in designing learner-centred environment. Each of these theories is based on the same underlying assumptions that learners are active agents purposefully seeking and contributing collaborative knowledge within a meaningful context. ICT offers various tools to implement above theories to create rich and engaging learning environments.

Modelling ICT Development in Education

Usefulness of Models

Countries in the Asia-Pacific region are at different stages of ICT development, in terms of both infrastructure and application of ICT in teaching and learning. Within any such country, there may be uneven development from region to region, area to area, and even from institution to institution. The Asia-Pacific region has a wide range of ICT development stages in education.

In view of the above considerations, it is useful to have a model for ICT development for developing competency standards for teacher development. Such a model can be a representation of the essential characteristics of ICT development to provide a scaffold or a framework. It can also be useful to show the inter-relationship of various components within a system and thus, help to locate its position in the whole framework. Models and frameworks can be useful in portraying how complex systems operate. Usually in visual form, they depict the major components in a system and the way these relate to each other. A framework for the integration of pedagogy and ICT in teacher education programmes, for instance, can show the major parts and the inter-relationship of these parts.

To the extent that such a framework reflects all that occurs, it may then serve as a blueprint that curriculum developers can take as a starting point in determining content, sequencing, and pedagogical process. A model has been presented that can be useful in determining the stage of ICT development reached by a country, a district, or even an individual institution. As mentioned earlier, this model is derived from international and national studies of ICT development that have identified a series of broad stages that educational system and institutions typically proceed through, in the adoption and use of ICT. The model is presented here to provide a framework for stages of pedagogy-technology integration.

The model conceives ICT development as a continuum along which an educational system or an individual institution can pinpoint the stage reached in the growth of ICT for their particular context. This model is referred to as a continuum of approaches to ICT development. The continuum model provides us with a holistic framework for identifying the needs for teacher development in different countries at different stages of development.

The Model

Studies of ICT development in both developed and developing countries identify at least four broad approaches through which educational systems and individual institutions typically proceed in their adoption and use of ICT. Sometimes, the number of stages identified varies. However, there is a general consensus that the introduction and use of ICT in education proceeds in broad stages that may be conceived as a continuum or series of steps.

Emerging Stage

Institutions at the initial stages of ICT development demonstrate the emerging approach. Such institutions have just started their journey in the ICT field with a skeleton computing infrastructure either donated or purchased by the institution authority. To start with, administrators and teachers just begin to explore the possibilities and consequences of using ICT for institutional management and adding ICT to the curriculum. Institutions at this emerging phase are still firmly grounded in traditional, teacher-centred practice.

The curriculum reflects an increase in learning how to acquire ICT basic skills such as office automation, e-mail and basic operation of computers, so that it prepares the ground for moving to the applying stage. In the emerging approach to ICT development, the focus is on the technical functions and uses of ICT and on the need for some knowledge and representation of the impacts of ICT on the system as a whole.

This approach often involves teachers' personal use of ICT, such as, the use of word processing to prepare worksheets, locating information on CD-ROMs or on the Internet, or communicating with friends and family by e-mail. Here, teachers are developing their ICT literacy and learning how to apply ICT to a range of personal and professional tasks. The emphasis is on training in a range of tools and applications, and increasing teachers' awareness of the opportunities for applying ICT to their teaching in the future.

Applying Stage

Those institutions, in which a new understanding of the

contribution of ICT to learning has developed, exemplify the applying approach. In this secondary phase, administrators and teachers use ICT for tasks already carried out in institutional management and in the curriculum. Teachers largely dominate the learning environment. Institutions at the applying approach phase adapt the curriculum in order to increase the use of ICT in various subject areas with specific tools and software such as drawing, designing, modelling and application of specific tools. This curriculum assists movement to the next stages, if so desired.

In the applying stage, teachers use ICT for professional purposes, focusing on improving their subject teaching in order to enrich how they teach with a range of ICT applications. This stage often involves teachers in integrating ICT to acquire specific subject skills and knowledge, beginning to change their teaching methodology in the classroom, and using ICT to support their training and professional development.

Teachers gain confidence in a number of generic and specialized ICT tools that can be applied to the teaching of their subject area. The opportunity to apply ICT in all their teaching is often limited only by a lack of ready access to ICT facilities and resources, which is why it is not fully integrated into all lessons for all students.

Infusing stage

At the third stage, the infusing approach involves integrating or embedding ICT across the curriculum, and is seen in those institutions that now employ a range of computer-based technologies in laboratories, classrooms, and administrative offices. Teachers explore new ways in which ICT changes their personal productivity and professional practice. The curriculum begins to merge subject areas to reflect real-world applications. In the infusing approach to ICT development, ICT infuses all aspects of teachers' professional lives in such ways as to improve student learning and the management of learning processes.

The approach supports active and creative teachers who are able to stimulate and manage the learning of students, integrating a range of preferred learning styles and uses of ICT in achieving their goals. The infusing stage often involves teachers easily integrating different knowledge and skills from other subjects into project-based curricula. In this approach, teachers fully integrate ICT in all aspects of their professional lives to improve their own learning, as well as, the learning of their students. Thus, they use ICT to manage not only the learning of their students but also their own learning. They use ICT to assist all students to assess their own learning in achieving specific personal projects. In this approach, it becomes quite natural to collaborate with other teachers in solving common problems and in sharing their teaching experiences with others.

Transforming Stage

Institutions that use ICT to rethink and renew institutional organization in creative ways are at the transforming approach. ICT becomes an integral, though invisible, part of daily personal productivity and professional practice. The focus of the curriculum is now learner-centred that integrates subject areas in real-world applications. ICT is taught as a separate subject at the professional level and is incorporated into all vocational areas. Institutions have become centres of learning for their communities.

In the transforming approach to ICT development, teachers and other staff members regard ICT as a natural part of the everyday life of the institutions that they begin to look at the process of teaching and learning in new ways. The emphasis changes from teacher-centred to learnercentred. Teachers, together with their students, expect a continuously changing teaching methodology designed to meet individual learning objectives.

Mapping the Model

The continuum model, as discussed in the previous section, can be mapped onto two interwoven tracks for the development of teachers' capacity in harnessing ICT with regard to (a) stages of ICT usage and (b) pedagogical usages of ICT.

Stages of ICT usage

Studies of teaching and learning in schools around the world identify four broad stages in the way that teachers and students learn about and gain confidence in the use of ICT. In the initial phase, teachers and learners become aware of ICT tools and their general functions and uses. In this stage, there is usually an emphasis on ICT literacy and basic skills. This stage of discovering ICT tools is linked with the emerging stage in ICT development.

Following on and from the first stage comes the stage of learning how to use ICT tools, and beginning to make use of them in different disciplines. This stage involves the use of general or particular applications of ICT, and is linked with the applying stage in the ICT development model.

The next stage is to understand how and when to use ICT tools to achieve a particular purpose, such as in completing a given project. This stage implies the ability to recognize situations where ICT will be helpful, choosing the most appropriate tools for a particular task, and using these tools in combination to solve real problems. This stage is linked with the infusing stage in the ICT development model.

The fourth and the last stage involves specializing in the use of ICT tools which occurs when one creates and transforms the learning environment with the help of ICT. This is a new way of approaching teaching and learning situation with specialized ICT tools and is linked with the transforming stage in the ICT development model.

Pedagogical Usages

Adoption of ICT in the classroom generally proceeds in four broad stages in the way the teachers and learners use ICT as a support to teaching and learning. These four stages give rise to the mapping depicted that have been broadly classified as supporting work performance, enhancing traditional teaching, facilitating learning and creating innovative learning environments, according to the stages of the proposed model. More than three decades ago, computers and related information technology were introduced to educators for direct teaching and learning purposes. ICT started its journey primarily with productivity tools, proceeded to self-learning courseware and multi-modal instruction, and finally progressed to web-based learning management system.

Supporting Work Performance

In the initial phase, teachers use productivity tools such as word processor, visual presentation software, spreadsheet, database, email etc., to support their daily work performance. During this stage, there is usually an emphasis on basic operations of electronic office software. This stage of using productivity tools for teaching and learning is linked with the emerging stage in ICT development.

ENHANCING TRADITIONAL TEACHING

Following on and from using productivity software, comes the stage of learning how to use and develop computer-assisted learning software and beginning to make use of such software in different disciplines. This stage involves the technique of integrating computer-based learning [3] in the traditional instructional process, and is linked with the applying stage in the ICT development model. Various instructional packages were selected, developed and used to enhance traditional classroom teaching.

Facilitating Learning

The next stage involves using various types of instructional software to facilitate student learning. The key point is that the teachers need to learn how to choose the most appropriate tools for a particular task, and using these tools in combination to solve real life problems. This stage implies the ability to recognize situations where various multimedia and specialized software can be utilized for teaching and learning. This stage is linked with the infusing stage in the ICT development model.

Creating innovative learning environments

The fourth and last stage involves specializing in the use of ICT to create an innovative learning environment that transforms the learning situation. This is possible by incorporating emerging trends in pedagogy and learning principles in teaching and learning. For this purpose, specialized software including modelling and simulation, expert systems, semantic networking etc., are employed to support pedagogical innovation. It helps to develop, deliver and manage open and flexible learning programme. This stage is linked with the transforming stage in the ICT continuum model.

Instructional Approaches

Adoption of ICT for varying instructional approaches with respect to complexity and authenticity of learning poses a complex inter-relationship. An attempt has been made for a three dimensional (or 3-D) representation of this complex inter-relationship between various instructional approaches. Such a representation is useful in defining ICT usage that might extend the learning potential of learners.

A Curriculum Framework for Integrating ICT and Pedagogy in Teacher Education

Frameworks, like models, do not have the property of being true or false. Rather, these may be useful, more useful, or perhaps not at all useful, for particular purposes

Every curriculum is a product of the environment in which it is positioned. This environment, called here contextual factors, includes three inter-related sets of factor: context, change, and lifelong learning.

The most obvious contextual factor within which any teacher education curriculum is planned is context. Context has a spatial dimension, which implies that it includes all the physical or environmental conditions about which curriculum planners need to be aware of. These include such factors as the economic conditions within a country, and the quality of the telecommunications infrastructure in place. Included as well are cultural and linguistic factors that arise, for instance, in consideration of whether particular software is appropriate or not. But context also has a temporal dimension, which implies that a particular curriculum is a product of time. As time changes, for instance, with changing political structures or demands in the workplace for new kinds of skill, the context changes.

This needs to be taken into account by curriculum planners.

Change

Change, and increasingly rapid change, characterizes modern societies. Driven by the revolution in ICT, new skills are required by the needs for an increasingly skilled workforce. This societal change, in turn, demands curriculum reforms in education systems around the world. It is this kind of change that the Delors Report of the International Commission on Education for the Twentyfirst Century identifies as creating tension between tradition and modernity. Change, then, is a key contextual factor in developing teacher education curricula. Clearly, leadership and vision are essential in planning and managing change, as is consideration of key stakeholders. In developing and implementing a curriculum to integrate ICT and pedagogy in teacher education, the UNESCO Planning Guide identifies who are the key stakeholders in the different sections within which a teacher education programme operates. These stakeholders include:

- the dean or professor with responsibility for teacher education
- the teaching staff in a programme of teacher education
- senior administrators in the institution
- pre-service teachers interested in acquiring ICT skills
- teachers and heads of institutions organizing field experiences for teachers in training
- government agencies that set policies for teacher professional development business and industries with an interest in the overall quality of graduates All stakeholders need to: (a) share a common vision

with respect to ICT; (b) modify the curriculum in teacher education; and (c) focus on making technology and sufficient resources available.

Lifelong learning

Lifelong learning, and indeed life-wide learning are other contextual factors since it is now recognized that learning does not stop after formal education ends. Again, the Delors Report recognized that learning throughout life is the only means to manage the tension between the extraordinary expansion of knowledge and capacity of human beings to assimilate it. The nature of ICT is one such change that curriculum planners need to build into teacher education curriculum, in order to enable budding teachers to continue their learning after graduating from the institution.

Teacher Competencies

The inner core of the teacher education curriculum pyramid comprises core teacher competencies, which are grouped into two major clusters of pedagogy and technology. These two clusters of teacher competencies, although discussed individually below, are not independent of each other in a curriculum where ICT is infused in pedagogical practice. As such, the basic philosophy of competencies of integration has also been highlighted separately.

Pedagogy

The UNESCO Planning Guide nominates pedagogy, along with content, as "the most important aspect of infusing technology in the curriculum". Infusion of ICT begins with teachers' mastery of the content of the subjects. With incorporation of ICT in teaching, teachers develop new ways of doing things, gradually changing the focus of classroom activities from an emphasis on teaching to an emphasis on learning.

As teachers become more familiar with ICT in the subjects, new ways of using ICT are explored so that their previous classroom delivery mechanism begins to change. In time, their classroom practice becomes transformed as the focus of the classroom becomes learner-centred and students use ICT to solve real-world problems that cut across traditional subject boundaries. Pedagogy includes much more. It includes theoretical knowledge and pedagogical skills. East China Normal University in Shanghai has developed a strong pre-service teacher education programme that focuses on educational uses of ICT and meaningfully integrates theory, pedagogical practice, and technology.

The key to the integrated curriculum approach at East China Normal University is, first, integrating on-campus training in ICT with field practice; second, integrating theoretical learning with pedagogical practice; and, third, integrating hands-on activities with minds-on activities -that is, learning by doing in combination with mental activities such as peer evaluation and self-reflection.

Pedagogy that further engages learners in critical thinking, creative thinking and problem solving skills is the core component of ICT integration. Whereas learning through facts, drill and practices, rules and procedures was more adaptive in earlier days, learning through projects and problems, inquiry and design, discovery and invention, creativity and diversity, action and reflection is more fitting now in the ICT-supported environment. Learning becomes constructivist, self-directed, flexible, interactive, deep and collaborative processing of knowledge.

Collaboration and networking are other aspects of pedagogy. The real power of ICT comes from new ways of communicating beyond the four walls of the classroom and by locating information from worldwide sources wherever these may be located. The implication for teachers as they assist their students in collaborating with other learning groups and using networks to research assignment topics is that they cease to be the main source of knowledge in the classroom. Instead, teachers' roles change from being "a sage on the stage" to becoming "a guide on the side". Teachers need to accommodate a philosophical shift in their approach to teaching. The UNESCO Planning Guide asserts that the development of teachers' competencies in collaboration and networking is essential to infusing ICT in the curriculum:

Through collaboration and networking, professional teachers promote democratic learning within the classroom and draw upon expertise both locally and globally.

Technology

Advances in technology and the way technology is incorporated into a system constitute a dynamic process. Each institution has to work within the context of its own system to fit choices to what best suits its unique situation and culture. The stages can be considered as hierarchical with the emerging stage as a starting point, and the transforming stage as a goal, which many perceive as the future of education. In the emerging stage, the focus is on the basic technical functions and uses of ICT. This stage involves teachers' competencies in word processing, spreadsheet, database, presentation software and uses of Internet and e-mail. Besides the kinds of ICT competencies relating to concepts and operations, there are many social, legal and ethical issues associated with the use of ICT about which teachers need to know. The facilities required to access information easily from remote sources, the ability to download it to a personal computer, and the utilization of the information in a classroom assignment, brings with it a host of social, legal, and ethical issues relating to copyright, evaluation of information sources, and appropriate forms of acknowledging electronic information.

In the applying stage, teachers use ICT for professional purposes, focusing on improving the teaching of subjects so as to enrich how to teach with a range of ICT tools. In the infusing stage, teachers infuse ICT in all aspects of professional life to improve student learning and the management of learning processes. ICT enables teachers to become active and creative in stimulating and managing the learning process, by infusing a range of preferred learning styles and uses of ICT in achieving educational goals. Teachers are required to master authoring tools, animation tools and multimedia tools to develop instructional software in different subjects.

The transforming stage is linked with schools that have used ICT creatively to rethink and renew school organization. ICT becomes an integral part of daily personal productivity and professional practice. The focus of the curriculum is now much more learner-centred and integrates subject areas in real-world applications, both in real and virtual environments. Teachers need to master special software, learning management system simulation and modelling tools, expert system, semantic networking and various web tools, in order to innovatively transform the teaching and learning system.

Although the approaches above are not a necessary hierarchical, these are intended to illustrate the steps towards growing ICT confidence and competence that many teachers go through, before beginning to transform teaching practice and the learning of their students.

Bearing in mind the contextual factors of change and lifelong learning, teachers are required to be competent in using new hardware and software. Technological competencies also have an attitudinal dimension. Cabanatan emphasized the importance of a positive attitude towards ICT and a clear understanding of the potential of ICT in education.

Integration

The inclusion of both pedagogy and technology as core competencies for teachers acknowledges that integrating ICT in education for teaching and learning is far broader than the simple acquisition of these two sets of competencies. Competencies of integration are neither competencies of technology alone nor are they competencies of pedagogy. Rather competencies of integration are about the appropriate selection, use, mix, fusion and integration of many sets of competencies including those covered under pedagogy and technology.

Teacher Education Curriculum

Having established a curriculum framework for teacher development in pedagogy-technology integration, a subsequent step is to begin the task of formulating the curriculum. The term curriculum implies the following:

— It refers to a contract between society, the State, and educational professionals with regard to educational experiences that learners should undergo during certain phases of their lives.

— It answers the why, what, when, where, how, and with whom the learning is to take place.

— It defines the foundations and content of education, their sequencing in relation to the amount of time available for the learning experiences planned, in terms of:

— methods to be used

— resources for learning and teaching, such as textbooks and new technologies, and

— evaluation.

Accordingly, pedagogy-technology integration forms an essential component of the overall curriculum for teacher education. As such, pedagogy-technology integration has to be referred to and even incorporated into the curriculum reforms for both pre-service teacher education as well as in-service teacher training in different countries of the Asia-Pacific region. In this way, all courses and subjects in teacher education/training programmes will be conducted on the basis of integrating ICT with curriculum.

The expected teachers graduated from universities will, therefore, be qualified for the teaching profession in new knowledge and lifelong learning society, while in-service teachers can be continuously trained and updated. In addition, the relationship between both curriculum reforms in basic education and teacher education need to be emphasized. This is mainly because of the current disparity between both these reforms. In some countries, curriculum reforms in basic education have gone ahead, but curriculum reforms for teacher education have lagged far behind, and this has had disadvantages for preparing tomorrow's teachers of the 21st century.

Competency Standards

A competency is a set of attributes covering knowledge, skills and attitudes for enabling one to effectively perform the activities of a given occupation or function to the standards expected in employment. The notion of competence with regard to the use of ICT in education is broader than the technical skills needed to use ICT. To take a technical view of competence is to deny the plethora of skills needed by teachers to create meaningful and productive learning contexts for learners. Therefore, whilst it may be easy to take a technical view of ICT competence, this is not sufficient to equip teachers to understand, and make effective use of, ICT in the classroom.

The type of ICT competence needed by teachers is a collection of knowledge, skills and attitudes that are inextricably bound up with the context and pedagogy. Competence needs to be embedded in teacher practices. A number of countries have developed national or regional ICT competency standards including Australia, Canada, People's Republic of China, India, New Zealand, United Kingdom and the United States.

Commonly, standards are developed first to describe what students have to do with ICT at different levels of schooling. Based on expected student outcome, a subsequent step is usually to describe what competencies their teachers are required to possess. In some cases, a further development is to create standards for educational administrators. All are particularly important to those who are responsible for providing pre-service and in-service teacher education. Competency standards can be stated either generally or quite specifically.

Curriculum Format

There is an important relationship between continuum models, curriculum frameworks and competency standards in ICT. When agreement is reached within a country or region for a curriculum framework for integrating ICT into learning, the development of competency standards for students and their teachers can follow. Furthermore, once a clear statement about ICT competency standards is arrived at, it is then possible to adapt or develop training modules for teachers.

Standards do not imply a prescribed course of study for all teachers across subject areas, nations, and regions. Generally, standards present a set of competencies that each local group of educators can interpret and translate into classroom practice based on their local context, the particular subject being taught, and their vision of ICT in education. While educators throughout the region share many common goals and beliefs about education, they come from different cultures.

These cultures dictate that calls for fuller integration of ICT into education are sensitive to these cultural differences. Change will not occur in the same manner in each nation or within different locations in any one nation. Competency standards, therefore, are often closely tied to local standards for students, so that expected student outcome in a particular field of study implies a set of competencies with ICT that their teachers should possess.

From the ICT continuum model, competency levels can be derived that reflect a teacher's continuous development of technology capability and pedagogical capability based on a curriculum framework. To be most effective, the ICT activities that a development programme provides are likely to deepen in complexity as a teacher's understanding and skills improve. The activities, therefore, have to be carefully designed to promote a teacher's movement into the next stage. Level-1 supports promote movement from stage 1 to stage 2, level-2 supports promote movement from stage 2 to stage 3, and level-3 supports promote movement from stage 3 to stage 4.

Each stage of the ICT development model characterizes the expertise the teacher is required to possess in pedagogy clusters, technology clusters and integration strategies. For example, teachers who are in the emerging stage are first becoming aware of the potential to use ICT in teaching and learning. The development programme might provide basic support through guidance by a mentor who helps these teachers to use ICT within their subject areas in simple but important ways.

This will encourage the movement of these teachers into the applying stage, in order to be engaged in more complex activities that promote deeper understanding. Here, the development programme might provide support through opportunities for discussion with colleagues doing similar work, or by providing collections of effective ICT infusions on a resource website. This encourages further growth into the infusing stage, when these teachers begin to apply knowledge and skills from other subjects into project based curricula. In the fourth and final stage i.e., transforming stage, teachers specialize in the use of ICT tools to create an innovative learning environment. This is a completely new way of approaching teaching and learning using ICT. In this stage, various software like experts systems, semantic networking, modelling and simulation etc., can be utilized to support innovative pedagogical approach.

Teachers just beginning to develop pedagogical skills are to be measured by standards represented by the emerging level of pedagogy. They progress through the standards as they further develop their skills. It is important to note that some teachers who have strong pedagogical skills and understanding may have limited skills with technology; for this, such teachers would be evaluated by the infusing standards in pedagogy, and the emerging standards in technology skills and integration strategies. Again, the standards for integration strategies at all levels have to reflect infusions of technology that support meaningful learning. With this approach, teachers are stimulated to develop through a natural progression implied by the standards, gaining both competence and confidence as they do so.

Why are such careful support strategies required? This is because teachers resist ICT innovations that do not match the context in which they work, but tend to integrate technology when it addresses real classroom problems, situations and learning goals. Teachers adapt to change when it is possible to set the goals, to have opportunities to acquire the needed skills, and to reflect on learning. It is the desire of teachers to infuse ICT directly into students' academic lives so that student activities are authentic and meaningful from the earliest stages. A similar approaches towards teacher training needs to be adopted.

Teachers are required to develop the simplest ICT skills in the midst of authentic teaching and learning activities that are seen as viable ways to solve existing professional and pedagogical problems. Teacher development is to be carefully planned, which is appropriate to a teacher's understanding and skills. This means that teachers learn to use ICT always within their zone of proximal development, so that activities are simple enough that teachers can place new ideas within the context of previous understanding, but are challenging enough to give their work meaning and purpose. Standards can play a key role in facilitating this kind of support.

Framework of Competency Standards

Based on the continuum model and support described above, competency levels can be identified and grouped into four major clusters. These four major clusters are categorized as (a) integrating productivity tools in learning context, (b) enhancing teaching and facilitating learning, (c) processing curriculum resources and learning materials, and (d) integrating ICT for pedagogical innovations encompassing the four stages in ICT development namely, emerging, applying, infusing and transforming stages.

This analytical framework of competency standards reflects that teachers' ICT-integrated competencies start with pedagogy. As teachers apply the latest technologies to enhance the effectiveness and efficiency of teaching, new questions are raised. From a pedagogical perspective, flexible use of technology is likely to facilitate teaching and learning. Teachers may choose different ways of using technology to achieve various learning objectives under different pedagogical philosophies. Technology use means methods or techniques to those who favour "teacher-centred" instructive theories; technology use might be more of a philosophy to those who favour "learner-centred" teaching theories, especially constructivism. Different educational viewpoints lead to different approaches and varied learning outcomes.

Teachers are not meant for operating as "sages on the stage" in this information age. Taking up roles as mentors, motivators, administrators, and designers of learning means sharing more responsibilities in promoting students' higher learning standards. They are expected to master and continually apply changing technology in the learning environment. When integrating technology into instruction, there have to be enough learning opportunities for teachers to equip themselves with the necessary skills.

It is critical to make teachers realize that incorporating technology into the fabric of classroom activities not only provides opportunities for teachers to enhance their teaching efficiency and effectiveness but also enables them to migrate from the traditional role of directing learning to a new role: facilitating learners to become self-directed. The stages of competency levels reflect teachers' continuous development and assume that from the earliest understanding and experience with ICT, teachers are working in an actual classroom context so that ICT is infused into teaching and learning.

Based on the analytical framework described above, an example of competency statements is proposed below, which consists of four major competency items under each cluster.

Cluster 1. Integrating productivity tools in learning practices

1.1 Demonstrate expertise in working with productivity tools that are applicable for teaching and learning work.

1.2 Design authentic and realistic tasks-based on pedagogical principles.

1.3 Demonstrate positive attitude in utilizing productivity tools for professional competence.

1.4 Demonstrating knowledge and skills of using ICT in ethical, legal and secure ways.

Cluster 2. Enhancing teaching and facilitating learning

2.1 Identify, plan and locate ICT resources to design and manage learner centred instruction and to support diverse needs of learners.

2.2 Demonstrate expertise with various instructional software development tools.

2.3 Design meaningful learning experiences and integrate interactive multimedia learning environments.

2.4 Apply ICT to facilitate a variety of assessment and evaluation strategies.

Cluster 3. Processing curriculum resources & learning materials

3.1 Demonstrate expertise in developing multi-modal resources using ICT to support curriculum.

3.2 Demonstrate expertises in developing web-based open and flexible learning (OFL) materials.

3.3 Stimulate and integrate learner directed research by using ICT to support knowledge construction.

3.4 Use ICT resources to collect, analyze, interpret and communicate findings to improve instructional practices.

Cluster 4. Integrating ICT for pedagogical innovation

4.1 Apply ICT to develop higher order skills and creativity.

4.2 Integrate ICT in meeting the needs of pedagogical innovations and learning strategies.

4.3 Employ specialized software tools to support pedagogical innovation.

4.4 Apply current research on teaching and learning with ICT while planning learning environment.

Infusions of Technology

Those responsible for teacher development may work with local teachers to create effective ICT infusions that are suitable to local context and specific curricula. Criteria like those given below, refined to the local context and subject area, may be used: (a) to evaluate and improve infusions as they are designed and applied during teacher development, and (b) for the teachers (and their supervisors) to use later as they begin to create infusions with their own students, so that they can evaluate and improve use of ICT within their own classroom context and practice.

These criteria help teachers think about the value of a learning activity. Activities that generally score well can be refined so that they are even better; those, which are poor, can be revised or abandoned. Again, the rubric can itself be adjusted and refined according to the local context. The types of assessment instrument used need to be sufficiently varied and flexible to enable competence to be demonstrated in a variety of ways reflecting the rich diversity of teaching and learning practice.

The assessment processes are required to be equitable and affordable so that all potential candidates have the same opportunities in terms of access to assessment. The nature of the assessment process needs to be made clear to all potential assessment candidates in terms of how it operates, what is expected from the candidates and how best to prepare. A mechanism for detailed feedback to all candidates requires to be established following completion of the assessment. Feedback has to be an integral part of the assessment process and with provision for including opportunities for further development. Involvement of all stakeholders in the assessment process is crucial for assessment of teacher professional standards.

Developing Capacity Building

Teachers constitute the largest professional group in most of the countries of the Asia-Pacific region: Ensuring continuing professional development of teachers presents a formidable challenge by itself. Integration of ICT into the various strategies for teaching and learning not only presents a new set of challenges, but also holds great opportunities that are intrinsic to the nature of the newer ICT. The rapid and inexorable movement towards a knowledge society places new demands on the knowledge, skills and competencies of teachers. At the same time, technology development gives rise to newer opportunities and advantages.

Applications of ICT have served to bridge temporal and spatial barriers that have long mitigated against introduction of new knowledge, approaches and techniques to teachers who work in far-flung areas. Productivity tools can give a teacher more time for professional growth and knowledge enrichment: this is over the time that is now spent on repetitive classroom management tasks. Accessing the global knowledge and information resources requires development of an environment that supports pedagogy-ICT integration at the national, local and institutional levels.

Optimal use of the knowledge tools and resources demands adequate preparation and skills of teachers in order to reap the maximum benefits of the emerging information society. The most important criterion for effective professional development is to tailor it to the learning needs and skill levels of individual teaching staff. This suggests that, ideally, an institution is required to, based on the availability of resources, provide a variety of options for professional development for the teachers. In structuring professional development options and resources, it is helpful to explore collaboration opportunities with partners outside the institution. The opportunities for ICT to create new paradigms of teaching and learning will depend largely on leadership and a shared vision, and on appropriate and continuing professional development.

There are three major components of capacity building objectives:

— The improvement of teachers' knowledge base, their skills and attitudes (KSA) in ICT integration

— The motivation of teachers to apply innovative pedagogical approaches and models in the classroom

— Making teachers competent in developing online/offline-learning resources.

Strategies Towards Professsional Development

Professional development refers to a variety of activities, both formal and informal, designed for the personal and professional growth of teachers with respect to pedagogy-technology integration. Professional development includes individual development, continuing education, in-service education or staff development, as well as, various professional developmental activities. It involves a wide variety of curricula to ensure that the teachers acquire and maintain the required competencies to face the diverse challenges of pedagogy-technology integration. It is concerned with the development of new insights into pedagogy and stimulates an on-going reflection into one's own practices.

Various professional development strategies exist for the successful implementation of pedagogy-technology integration. The strategies recognize the diversity within the region in terms of culture, languages and ethnicity. They encourage innovative practices. The strategies also focus on incorporating ICT development, education reforms and professional development of teachers in national policies and plans.

National plans and programmes require taking into account teachers' needs and concerns, particularly those related to their professional development. Commitment and support at various levels (facilitators, policy makers, communities and other stakeholders) are crucial in facilitating successful implementation of any national policy. Teachers may find it impossible to incorporate ICT into their work without support from peers, parents, leaders and other stakeholders. To bring this about, these community members may also need professional development along with the teachers. Countries that have initiated efforts to infuse ICT into teacher education have found the following professional development strategies to be helpful in successful technology integration:

a) Professional development programme on ICT integration places pedagogy over technology. The focus lies in teaching and learning rather than hardware and software alone. In other words, it is not only about mastering ICT skills but also utilizing ICT to improve teaching and learning.

b) Professional development of teachers requires adequate access to ICT resources in the classroom. The better the access to ICT, the more likely it will be used for in structional purposes. This is a big challenges across the Asia-Pacific region because of the diversity of institutions and the difference in resources.

c) A 'Just in Time' (JIT) approach to professional development is a model that works well. In this approach, professional development is provided to teachers on a as-and-when-required basis.

d) Capacity building is a sustained, continuing and lifelong process. It is not a one-time activity. Teachers need to update their knowledge and skills as the school curriculum and technology change. Individuals develop in stages and mature over time.

e) Professional development is a building process. Preferably it starts with what teachers do well in the classroom. Teachers can then gradually build their skills and knowledge in successive steps, towards pedagogy-technology integration.

f) Capacity building should be based on learning needs and skills of individuals. A detailed needs assessment is essential in order to identify gaps between the present status and the target to be achieved.

g) ICT has the potential to break the professional isolation from which many teachers suffer. ICT provides a suitable means of connectivity with universities, peers, mentors, centres of excellence and the sources of teaching and learning materials. While developing professional development strategies, one requires to take into account the following guiding principles to promote pedagogy-ICT integration in its proper context:

— Infuse ICT into the entire teacher education programme: pre-service, in-service, and both formal and informal teacher education.

— Integrate ICT in all activities of education: teaching, learning and administration.

— Empower teachers to develop knowledge, skills and positive attitudes actively towards integrating ICT in teaching and learning.

— Integrate ICT in all aspects of learning, and in all phases of the learning process.

— Integrate ICT for lifelong learning.

— Innovate ICT to embody and model the forms of pedagogy that teachers can use themselves in their classrooms.

— Apply hands-on, learner-centred principles in designing professional development programme.

— Use ICT for empowering teachers to use a variety of learning strategies.

— Apply ICT to promote higher order thinking skills.

— Emphasize the professional development of teachers to reduce the digital divide within and among the member/participating countries.

— Use ICT to remove barriers between learners and facilitators.
— Provide an authentic learning environment for ICT integration.
— Encourage teachers to be mentors, tutors, guides and facilitators.
— Encourage self-directed learning independent of space and time.

Approaches to Capacity Building

There is a variety of approaches to capacity building and an overview of the approaches may prove to be helpful in determining the specific requirements of each country in the context of diverse environments in the region. The various planning guides adopted by the different countries suggest a number of useful approaches for high quality professional development programmes. Some of these are discussed below:

1. Professional development programmes respect and encourage the leadership development of teachers. There is a variety of such roles including mentoring new teachers, acting as consulting teachers, coordinating alliances and networks among teachers, and doing advocacy work etc.
2. A balance between collaborative work and individual learning is required. Central to the professional development enterprise is a learning culture that is collaborative. Examples of collaborative activities are joint planning, problem solving, study groups, team teaching, and participation in alliance.
3. Accountability and evaluation of professional development programmes provide a basis for future planning. All professional development plans have

to be evaluated against data about student learning, institutional needs and goals, and teaching and content standard.

Inadequate training is one of the major obstacles to the effective use of ICT in teaching and learning. If teachers do not not receive adequate training at the pre-service stage, the learning gaps may be filled through in-service training. The development of ICT influences two important aspects of delivering professional training programmes. One is the way the institutions train prospective teachers and the other is how institutions design continuing education for teachers to learn on-the-job either at the physical workplace or through virtual learning. There are various merits and demerits of different approaches of professional development programmes.

A popular strategy for delivering professional programmes is to provide centralized training offered through direct contact mode. This has limited success unless followed up by training and support for the effective use of ICT by trained teachers. Another useful approach to professional development is school-based training. School-based training is an on-site, customized teacher-training programme for in-service teachers. The training course is arranged in a small group of maximum twenty persons that ranges in duration from 2 to10 days, depending on the content.

Several organizations such as the Institute for Teacher Education: In-Service Department (UK, Australia), the Princess Sirindhorn IT Project (Thailand), and World Links (funded by the World Bank in various countries) use this approach with their teacher training projects. According to these sources, institution-based training approach is cost-effective. Some factors based on experiences regarding on-site training from Australia,

Maldives, Thailand, United Kingdom and the United States are the need for:

— teacher reform policy-putting the emphasis from teacher training organizations to institutions
— teachers' initiative for professional development
— team-work building
— familiarizing teachers with computer equipment at the institution

It is difficult for teachers to take time out from their regular teaching schedules to attend extended training courses; therefore, providing on-site training at their institutions is more convenient and specific to their needs. Successful models for professional development reflect the holistic nature of capacity building rather than focusing only on technological skills. Mentoring and reciprocal mentoring is an example of a professional development model that builds capacity within an organization.

In the early stages of this process, many teachers develop confidence in working with ICT from the primary level and slowly keep pace with growing confidence and autonomy. ICT has increased the access and flexibility to reach learners any time and anywhere. Mentorship can be fostered across geographical boundaries by using synchronous and asynchronous interaction. Training programmes can be organized for intensive face-to-face sessions, followed by long term follow-up, using online learning strategies. This hybrid approach to capacity building is becoming popular in most of the developing countries. Apart from the face-to-face, on-site institution-based training, online training and direct mentoring methods, there are various other capacity building exercises. They include:

- — exchange programme
- — workshop at local, regional, national and international levels
- — case study
- — web-based learning
- — self-directed instructional resources including multimedia packages

While the potential of technology to offer creative opportunities for individual and collaborative learning for teachers is no longer debated, the realities of education in the developing countries in the region include the fact that computers in institutions are inadequate, connectivity is still limited and most other technology resources are unevenly distributed. Can ICT in this context still promote the best practices of professional development? The following show examples of ways in which teachers can make optimum use of ICT for professional development.

1. Teachers of the same subject area can take turns researching on professional development issues or topics that could be discussed, articles could be downloaded, indexed, hyper-linked to actual sites and saved in staff development folders for using offline.
2. A small number of computers may be set aside exclusively for professional development purposes. Departmental committees may be formed to determine the web-based resources related to ICT integration for professional development purposes.
3. Copies of files and folders of professional development articles and web-based resources can be made available on CDs to rural schools that have no Internet connectivity.

4. Use of an intranet system, which features a discussion or "knowledge forum", can be a useful approach for professional development. Young teachers may seek assistance from experienced teachers by posting questions relating to ICT integration. Teachers can join online study groups where connectivity is strong in order to explore better ways of teaching and sharing experiences.
5. Videos of lessons demonstrating seamless technology infusion in various subject areas can be viewed and critiqued by teachers during staff development meetings.
6. Visits to institutions that have rich pedagogy-technology environments can help to understand and benchmark ICT integration.

An institution can adopt or develop a competency continuum for pedagogy-ICT integration. Based on this, individual professional growth plan of a teacher can be benchmarked. Teacher training institutions, professional societies, institutional administrators and educational policy makers continue to identify, study and disseminate examples of pedagogy-ICT integration that respond to professional needs.

Teachers may find it impossible to incorporate ICT into their work without support from peers, parents, leaders and other stakeholders of the education system. To bring this about, there is a need to form a support group comprising parents, local business groups, NGOs, and the community at large with teachers at the core to facilitate integration of ICT into the teaching and learning system. This will create a local knowledge base for infusing ICT integration. This local knowledge needs to be integrated with regional and international knowledge base of ICT for teacher development.

Regional and international collaboration can provide ongoing mentoring and support for those who lead ICT in teacher education within and outside institutions. They engage in discussions on topics more relevant to their needs and practices such as ways of customizing software to local contexts. Such collaborative problem solving among the countries within the region and outside is important to many teachers who have relatively little access to technical support or opportunities to view new developments.

Knowledge can be availed of, extended, shared and transformed using knowledge portals and gateways. Global gateways provide a necessary filter to help reduce information overload. Even more importantly, the filtered information has been evaluated before placement in a portal, and often links to sources and resources are accompanied by brief descriptions. Like the rapid growth in information, the number of web portals has similarly increased and so also guide to online knowledge networks. The large store of resources at a particular portal is easy to navigate and useful for capacity building. The ICT portal for teachers developed by UNESCO Asia and Pacific Regional Bureau for Education is one example [4]. There is a strong need to develop online teacher resource bases in the area of pedagogy-technology integration at national levels and link them with the portals at regional levels. Content development, teacher designed e-lesson plans, knowledge base on ICT integration and various innovative practices can be shared for effective use of ICT to improve teaching and learning. The best innovative approaches and high quality teaching materials produced by the teachers call for reward and encouragement.

Based on experiences, offline networks can be developed in centres of excellence such as universities, research centres and teacher training institutions. In this context, it has to be emphasized that an inquiry system that helps teachers find the right resources, at the right time, for the right audience, etc., easily and efficiently, is required to be set up for online knowledge resources in order to ensure optimal use of the resource base.

Implications for Professional Development

ICT has provided a new perspective and opportunity to motivate and engage teachers in professional development programmes. ICT can contribute significantly to all the three components of professional development:

Firstly, it can bring world experiences into professional training by providing good teaching and learning materials, facilitating simulations and capturing and analyzing best practices of teaching.

Secondly, ICT can open a world of flexible lifelong professional development programme by offering training any time and anywhere.

Finally, ICT can break the professional isolation of teachers by connecting them in a virtual network and with valuable resources of teaching and learning materials. Unless teachers are given due recognition for the key role that they can play and thus encourage them towards innovation, the transformation level of ICT integration becomes a harder target to reach. In order to create successful programme for capacity building and for teachers to become pioneers, inventors and shapers of the new culture of learning, professional development programmes should consider the following elements:

— inspire teachers to invent

— focus on experiential learning

— conduct need assessments

— provide greater opportunities for feedback and reflections

— improve teacher competence in ICT integration

Issues and Strategies

It is important in leadership to establish and articulate a clear vision toward change. It is helpful, as one can seek a profound shift in the way teachers approach their craft, to continually remind them and oneself of what it looks like when active, motivated students use technology in a meaningful way.

With the help of the Internet, students embarked on a virtual field trip to a Natural History Museum about three thousand miles away. After touring exhibits, students interviewed and questioned experts and curator via two-way video conferencing. As students broke into teams to study specific species, teacher guided and managed their individual research and learning plans.

One group of students narrowed their investigation to ants. Unlike hundreds of students of a particular teacher over the years who simply drew pictures to memorize ant anatomy, these students used an animation simulator. With this tool, the students created a three-dimensional moving ant model. When they forgot to include all the limbs, their creation hobbled jerkily. This humorously reinforced basic facts about movement and structure. In the field, members of the team carried hand-held personal digital assistance to record and send data regarding the population, habitat, soil quality and moisture levels instantaneously via their wireless connection to the Internet. The four collaborators back at the institution built and organized their findings into a database. This gave a baseline to compare and analyze their findings against those from other parts of the world.

As the group searched for a more original way to report on the ants' activities, the teacher gave expert guidance as to how to record video clips with footage using video editing software. The entire class voted to include these video clips, built up a web page and shared their profiles with students of China. E-mail correspondence with China generated not only surprising information about the different kinds of red ants living in China, but also knowledge of Chinese cultural traditions.

Thus, digital learning integrates technology, connectivity, content and human resources. Otherwise, the students would have listened passively to a particular teacher standing in front of a classroom and describing the anatomy of ants and showing a drawing on blackboard. One can name several attributes of meaningful learning that are evident in this example: students are actively engaged with the material, are doing an authentic task in the field that is intrinsically interesting, and are collaborating as they do so. It is helpful for the leadership to have a number of examples of this kind of learning, which are always available to illustrate the vision of ICT integration, and to inspire others to reach for it.

ICT has provided a large array of tools and environment to implement instructional techniques that address divergent or creative thinking of learners. Various software now exist to-nurture curiosity, openness to experience, broad interest, originally, imaginative play, intuition, attraction to novelty, artistic ability, metaphorical thinking, problem solving, elaboration of ideas and breaking away from norms-all of which are attributes of creative people. It will be the responsibility of teachers to help learners think critically and develop understanding through the use of appropriate ICT tools.

Structures for Implementation

A central feature of this approach is the development of

focused, multi-disciplinary teams at the local level that will help teachers and students infuse technology meaningfully into academic activities. A team assigned to each subject area can assist teachers to more fully integrate technology into learning of that discipline. The teams can be modelled after the overall regional and national level teams that develop a coherent strategy and a set of guidelines for ICT, create sample lesson plans in core subjects, and conduct a series of training workshops and online courses, each potentially discipline-specific. This way, the team is effectively replicated throughout the region with following objectives:

— Engage teachers in activities during subject area preparation and teacher assignments so that they develop the skills to use technology effectively in their classrooms.

— Provide technical support, instructional support, incentives, and ongoing development for in-service teachers to help them effectively practise and model technology integration.

— Investigate meaningful infusions for each discipline, refining and adopting those that seem most effective.

Encourage teachers within and between disciplines to collaborate on meaningful instructional uses of technology and to share problems, strategies and solutions. This modelling and support will encourage teachers to develop their own innovative models and practices. Local teams work to create or adapt infusions for the target teachers and subject areas, and will consider local factors such as resources, infrastructure, curricula, student characteristics, and teacher practices. This will ensure that the infusions are suitable for the people involved and are likely to support meaningful learning in their community context.

By working locally, the teams are likely to devise unique, innovative infusions that are custom designed for specific contexts. The local teams will have overall responsibility for evaluating the extent to which the infusions succeed, and for providing ongoing support for the teachers. At the same time, there will be conventional approaches to training such as institution-based face-to-face training followed by on-site institution-based training, direct mentoring and online training. The mode of the training programme will depend on the context and cultural tradition of the country. Whatever be the mode, the training has to emphasize hands-on-practice and inquiry-based learning, modelling the pedagogy that teachers can employ in their classrooms.

Development of resource materials

The Resource Kit is a valuable collection comprising various media: videos of classroom practice, audio interviews with teachers on cassette, sample lesson plans and teaching modules on CD-ROM, and printed materials. The diverse teaching and learning materials contained in the Resource Kit will be collected in-house, continually expanded and refined over a period of time, and packaged in a convenient form for use. It can be promoted as a resource for teacher educators at regional workshops and at international meetings in the region.

E-resources for teacher development

A number of the e-resources produced by UNESCO Asia and Pacific Regional Bureau for Education on training and professional development of teachers are available on CD-ROM. Building on these promising starts, additional e-resources for teacher educators might include a range of materials in electronic format such as-policy documents, reports and databases, multimedia courseware, online educational journals, electronic books, newspapers online, glossaries, and online tools.

Along with the Internet, provision has to be made to create master CD-ROMs for distributing e-resources to every educational institution in the Asia-Pacific region. E-resources for teacher educators would contain copyright-free resource materials, together with links to other freely available online resources so that, wherever an Internet connection is available, teacher educators would enjoy access to a library of information that had been already been evaluated, filtered, and judged useful.

As with other products generated, e-resources for teacher educators could be promoted at regional workshops, international conferences, and through UNESCO's Regional Clearinghouse on ICT in Education for Asia and the Pacific. Besides, an introductory packet containing e-resources together with a rationale and value statements that help the stakeholders learn about integrating ICT can be made available to users at national, local and individual levels which would go a long way in implementing ICT integration.

Approaches to Successful Impelementation

Teaching through technology portfolio

Participating teachers have to develop and maintain a "Teaching through Technology Portfolio" as a means to document and reflect on their own learning and to provide evidence of success. The portfolios form an integral component of the regularly scheduled sharing sessions with the peers and team leaders.

Examples of content are:

— lesson plans used to facilitate technological support for learning in curricular areas

— assessment and measurement strategies in particular curricular areas
— evaluation strategies and uses of evaluation information in particular curricular areas
— measures of student achievement/performance
— critical Incident Logs that focus on increased content knowledge
— peer observations and feedback on technological support for learning
— affective measures of student perceptions of use of technology

Bibliography

Bailey, K. and Nunan, D., eds., *Voices from the Language Classroom*, Cambridge: CUP, 1996.

Bolitho, R. and Tomlinson, B. 2nd ed, *Discover English*, Oxford: Heinemann, 1995.

Doff, A., *Teach English: A training course for teachers*, Cambridge: CUP, 1988.

Flowerdew, J., Brock, M. and Hassiya, S., eds., *Perspectives on Second Language Education*, Hong Kong: City Polytechnic of Hong Kong, 1992.

Freeman, D. and Richards, J., eds., *Teacher Learning in Language Teaching*, Cambridge: CUP, 1996.

Hayes, D., ed., *In-service Teacher Development: International perspectives*, Hemel Hempstead, Herts.: Prentice Hall, 1997.

Head, K. and Taylor, P., *Readings in Teacher Development*, Oxford: Heinemann, 1997.

Li, D., Mahoney, D., and Richards, J., eds., *Exploring Second Language Teacher Development*, Hong Kong: City Polytechnic of Hong Kong, 1994.

McGrath, I., ed., *Learning to Train*, Hemel Hempstead, Herts.: Prentice Hall, 1997.

Parrott, M., *Tasks for Language Teachers*, Cambridge: CUP, 1993.

Richards, J. and Nunan, D., eds., *Second Language Teacher Education*, Cambridge: CUP, 1990.

Roberts, J., *Language Teacher Education*, London: Edward Arnold, 1998.

Sadtono, E., ed., *Language Teacher Education in a Fast Changing World*, Singapore: SEAMO Regional Language Center, 1992.

Sadtono, E., ed., *Issues in Language Teacher Education*, Singapore: SEAMO Regional Language Center, 1992

Spratt, M., *English for the Teacher*, Cambridge: CUP, 1994.

Tanner, R. and Green, C., *Tasks for Teacher Education*, Harlow, Essex: Addison Wesley Longman, 1998.

Sachs, G., Brock, M. and Lo, R., eds., *Directions in Second Language Teacher Education*. Hong Kong: City Polytechnic of Hong Kong, 1996.

Trappes-Lomax, H. and McGrath, I., eds., *Theory in Language Teacher Education*, Harlow, Essex: Longman, 1999.

Ur, P., *A Course in Language Teaching*, Cambridge: CUP, 1996.

Wajnryb, R., *Classroom Observation Tasks*, Cambridge: CUP, 1992.

Wallace, M., *Training Foreign Language Teachers: A reflective approach*, Cambridge: CUP, 1991.

______________., *Action Research for Language Teachers*, Cambridge: CUP.

Woodward, T., *Models and Metaphors in Language Teacher Training*, Cambridge: CUP, 1991.

______________., *Ways of Training*, Harlow, Essex: Longman, 1992.

______________., *Ways of Working with Teachers*, Kent: TW Publications, 2004.

Index